Samuel P. Wiggins

during World War II. He was in South Korea in 1961-62 as Chief Adviser of a Project in Teacher Education. He was selected as a Fulbright lecturer in South America for duties in the summer of 1966 with the Association of Colombian Universities.

Professor Wiggins is the author of *Southern High Schools and Jobless Youth* (1961), *Battlefields in Teacher* Education (1964), two college texts, and numerous professional articles. The author is director of the Southern Higher Education Study of George Peabody College for Teachers, established by a subvention from the General Education Board. This volume and the major publication to follow it, *Higher Education in the South,* report upon studies made possible by that grant.

THE DESEGREGATION ERA
IN HIGHER EDUCATION

THE DESEGREGATION ERA
in
HIGHER EDUCATION

SAM P. WIGGINS, Director
Southern Study in Higher Education

Supported by a grant from the General Education Board
to George Peabody College for Teachers

McCutchan Publishing Corporation
2526 Grove Street
Berkeley, California 94704

Foreword

Peter P. Muirhead

Associate Commissioner for Higher Education
Office of Education
U.S. Department of Health, Education, and Welfare

This is a timely book on an important problem.

Since the Civil Rights Act of 1964 it has been the desegregation of elementary and secondary schools which has been in the public eye. Mr. Wiggins' book reminds us again of the extent of changes which have taken place in southern colleges and universities since 1948, and more particularly since the Supreme Court decision of May 17, 1954.

He views the "era of desegregation" as a period now almost over, which is distinguished by the achievement of the limited goal of assured access of Negroes to historically white, segregated institutions. This book is largely concerned with describing the extent of that achievement and its meaning, forming a basis for the author's recommendations on the requirements of further progress toward what he calls "a true ethnic community in higher education all across America."

As Director of the Southern Study in Higher Education Mr. Wiggins has direct knowledge of a wide variety of southern institutions and of research on desegregation in the South in progress and completed. From such a background of understanding and scholarship, it is reassuring to note that he supports the thesis that the higher education community and the southern regional educational associations and foundations are rapidly getting beyond questions of desegregation to the basic questions of total educational production.

This is a constructive book. It is particularly welcome in its implication that a willingness in principle to desegregate does not in itself fulfill either the letter or the spirit of the Civil Rights Act, and that progress beyond this point to a full application of democratic principles, wherever it may be needed, demands our earnest and thoughtful attention.

TO THE READER

"Some men have been virtuous blindly, others have speculated fantastically, and others have been shrewd to bad purposes; but you, sir, I am sure will give under your hand, nothing but what is at the same moment, wise, practical, and good."

Letter to Mr. Benjamin Franklin from Mr. Benjamin Vaughan, dated January 1, 1783, and quoted in the commemorative edition of *The Autobiography of Benjamin Franklin* (Boston: Houghton Mifflin and Company, 1906), p. 77. —From this assumption, the author proceeds.

THE AUTHOR'S PREFACE

In the summer of 1963, a concern was felt throughout the southern regions about some of the prevalent problems in southern higher education, those not limited to, but predominantly characteristic of the South. The problems formed a kind of endemic cluster, consisting of those associated frequently with race, those related to poverty, and those growing out of educational disadvantages among both Negro and white youth. The General Education Board, with a sympathetic concern about the varied human problems within the South, made a generous subvention of $115,000 to George Peabody College for Teachers to conduct studies relating to this cluster of problems. The major study, under the title *Higher Education in the South*, will be published in the fall of 1966.

In developing the major report, a need was felt for a briefer treatise concerning the desegregation era in higher education, because of its immediate import to all of America. The recent past is of considerable significance to us now to the extent that it can guide us in giving shape to the future. This minor report, then, focuses on a kind of social history of the accelerated evolution of desegregation in southern colleges and universities. The report concludes with a realistic, hopeful look to the kind of future that is within our collective grasp as we try to be "at the same moment, wise, practical, and good."

Data have been gathered from a variety of sources by the author and by the Assistant Director of the Southern Higher Education Study, Dr. Harold N. Stinson. Together and separately, we have visited dozens of southern colleges and universities and have interviewed scores of administrators, students and professors throughout the southeastern quadrant of America. A list of those institutions follows this prefatory statement. Beyond our extended interviews, we have had the benefit, in opinionnaire form, of the reflective judgments of the presidents of numerous southern colleges not listed among the visited institutions.

In conducting this and the major study, we have been indeed fortunate in obtaining the counsel of an Advisory Board of individuals who are well-informed about various aspects of southern life and thought, and especially about southern higher education. The advisors have been generous with their time, and exceedingly helpful in their constructive criticism of flaws within this study. With reference to the present report, Mr. Reed Sarratt, former Executive Director of the Southern Education Reporting Service, and present Director of the Journalism Project of the Southern Regional Education Board, has been of invaluable help in making data available for our use. As a member of the board, his mature interpretation of data and his judgments have been consistently helpful. Mr. Jim Leeson, Director of Information and Research of the Southern Education Reporting Service, has been of inestimable help in many of our fact-gathering efforts.

The author is indebted to Dr. Guy B. Johnson, Kenan Professor of Sociology at the University of North Carolina and co-editor of *Social Forces*, whose pioneering studies in this area more than a decade ago enabled us to supply facts where only conjecture would otherwise have been possible. We are indebted to Dr. R. E. Cleary, Associate Professor of Political Science at the American University and recent Congressional Fellow of the U. S. House of Representatives, for his unpublished working paper on "Gubernatorial Politics and Southern Higher Education," prepared expressly for our use. In the legal dimension of this report, timely assistance has been received from Dr. Jerre S. Williams, the Rex G. Baker Professor of Law at the University of Texas School of Law.

Mrs. Shirley Williams, a graduate assistant with the Southern Study, has been helpful in a variety of ways, including the development of recommendations growing out of this investigation. Mrs. Faye Reedy, staff secretary, has shown the spirited enthusiasm of youth and an unfailing dependability throughout the numerous revisions of this report.

Most of all, gratitude is expressed to those students, professors, deans, and presidents who have reflected in confidential interviews an unselfish commitment to a lawful society and an active concern for a new relevancy of higher education in America. Their honest efforts to study new social forces mark them as leaders in a post-desegregation era, and generate new hope that ethnic congeniality may yet be achieved in higher education in our time.

The freedom associated with the writing of this report has carried a humbling responsibility to work in the social interest, and leaves none else responsible for the shortcomings of the study but its director, the author of this report. The report is, in its final form, one man's views of the desegregation era as he has been helped to see it by many others who have generously shared their data, their time, and their varied perceptive judgments in the interest of societal progress.

Sam P. Wiggins

The Advisory Board
Southern Study in Higher Education

Mr. Donald C. Agnew, Director
Educational Improvement Project
Southern Association of Colleges and
 Schools
Atlanta, Georgia

Mr. William C. Archie, Dean
College of the Arts and Sciences
The University of Delaware
Newark, Delaware

Mr. Howard R. Boozer, Director
State Board of Higher Education
Raleigh, North Carolina

Mr. A. H. Calloway, Director
Information Service
West Virginia State College
Institute, West Virginia

Mr. Rufus Clement, President
Atlanta University
Atlanta, Georgia

Mr. Milton Cummings, President
Brown Engineering Company
Huntsville, Alabama

Mr. R. P. Daniel, President
Virginia State College
Petersburg, Virginia

Mr. Frank Dickey, Executive Director
National Commission on Accrediting
Washington, D. C.

Mr. Curtis Dixon
National Representative
Woodrow Wilson National Fellowship
 Foundation
Atlanta, Georgia

Mr. Luther Foster, President
Tuskegee Institute
Tuskegee, Alabama

Mr. Winfred Godwin, Director
Southern Regional Education Board
Atlanta, Georgia

Mr. Rufus Harris, President
Mercer University
Macon, Georgia

Mr. Herman Long, President
Talladega College
Talladega, Alabama

Mr. Hugh McEniry, Dean
Stetson University
DeLand, Florida

Mr. John Popham, Managing Editor
The Chattanooga Times
Chattanooga, Tennessee

Mr. Felix C. Robb, President
George Peabody College for Teachers
Nashville, Tennessee *and*
Director-elect, Southern Association
 of Colleges and Schools

Mr. Reed Sarratt, Director
Journalism Project
Southern Regional Education Board
Atlanta, Georgia

Mr. A. B. Templeton, President
Sam Houston State College
Huntsville, Texas

Mr. Bernard Werthan, Sr., President
Werthan Bag Corporation
Nashville, Tennessee
(Trustee, Peabody College)

Mr. Stephen Wright, President
Fisk University
Nashville, Tennessee

Miss Flora Rhind (Unofficial)
Special Assistant to the President
The Rockefeller Foundation
New York, New York

Southern Colleges and Universities Visited in Connection with the Southern Higher Education Study, 1964–65

Alabama A and M College
  Huntsville, Alabama
Arkansas A, M, and N College
  Pine Bluff, Arkansas
Armstrong College
  Savannah, Georgia
Atlanta University
  Atlanta, Georgia
Auburn University
  Auburn, Alabama
Augusta College
  Augusta, Georgia
Berea College
  Berea, Kentucky
Birmingham Southern College
  Birmingham, Alabama
Clemson University
  Clemson, South Carolina
Fairmont State College
  Fairmont, West Virginia
Fisk University
  Nashville, Tennessee
Florida A and M University
  Tallahassee, Florida
Florida State University
  Tallahassee, Florida
Fort Valley State College
  Fort Valley, Georgia
Georgia Southern College
  Statesboro, Georgia
George Washington University
  Washington, D. C.
Grambling College
  Ruston, Louisiana
Jackson State College
  Jackson, Mississippi
Kentucky State College
  Frankfort, Kentucky
Little Rock University
  Little Rock, Arkansas
Louisiana Polytechnic Institute
  Ruston, Louisiana
Louisiana State University at
  New Orleans
  New Orleans, Louisiana
Memphis State University
  Memphis, Tennessee

Mercer University
  Macon, Georgia
Miles College
  Birmingham, Alabama
Millsaps College
  Jackson, Mississippi
Northeast Louisiana State College
  Monroe, Louisiana
Oakwood College
  Huntsville, Alabama
Paine College
  Augusta, Georgia
Philander Smith College
  Little Rock, Arkansas
Rice University
  Houston, Texas
Savannah State College
  Savannah, Georgia
Scarritt College
  Nashville, Tennessee
Southern University
  Baton Rouge, Louisiana
Southwest Texas State College
  San Marcos, Texas
Texas Southern University
  Houston, Texas
Tougaloo College
  Tougaloo, Mississippi
Trinity University
  San Antonio, Texas
Union College
  Barbourville, Kentucky
University of Arkansas Medical
  School
  Little Rock, Arkansas
University of Mississippi
  Oxford, Mississippi
University of Tennessee
  Knoxville, Tennessee
University of Texas
  Austin, Texas
Vanderbilt University
  Nashville, Tennessee
West Virginia State College
  Institute, West Virginia
Wood Junior College
  Mathiston, Mississippi

Contents

1. The Cake of Custom

In a "stump dotted clearing" in Ohio two young missionaries resolved, in 1833, to found a college on what was then the western frontier, "to train teachers and other Christian leaders for the boundless and most desolate fields in the West."[1] The following year, forty-four students began classes at the Oberlin Collegiate Institute, attesting to the action-oriented resolve of these two men with vision. In 1835, the trustees established a policy of admitting students "irrespective of color," and Oberlin came to be the "first college to declare its instruction open to all races."[2]

Berea College, in Kentucky, was subsequently founded in that tradition, with some influence from Oberlin College. Students were admitted to Berea's first freshman class, in 1869, without reference to creed or color. Berea faced problems, however, that Oberlin never knew. Beginning as a one-room district school in 1855, it was coerced into discontinuance in 1859 because of the antislavery ideas cultivated there. Berea resumed operation on a precollegiate level in 1866, and with its college freshman class of 1869, the principle of desegregation hesitantly moved South. The Kentucky legislature intervened in 1904, forbidding the practice of desegregation to continue. Since the 1890 Constitution prohibited desegregation in public higher education, it was felt that private institutions of higher learning should also be governed by that restriction. By a legal amendment in 1950, however, Berea College resumed its historic policy and practice of admitting students without reference to ethnic origin.[3]

These examples of pioneering effort in higher education suggest a number of principles related to social change in general and to desegregation in particular, but it would be premature to attempt their identification here. At that time, the Oberlin and Berea colleges seemed to be

1

isolated events in the stream of history. The tribulations of Berea College illustrate well the concept of the "Cake of Custom," given that label by the sociologist Walter Bagehot. This was his way of explaining the social behavior which places a moral obligation on conformity to custom. There was then, and is now, a social penalty attached to nonconformity.

But, within prescribed limits, nonconformity was permitted even within the deep South. Tougaloo College, a predominantly Negro college established in Jackson, Mississippi in 1869, has since its founding provided a singular instance of faculty desegregation in a predominantly Negro institution in the deep South. For generations, this policy of desegregation remained in effect, unpublicized and relatively undisturbed.

Despite these and a few other instances of desegregated higher learning, the seal of segregation remained intact in the South a hundred years after the founding of Oberlin Collegiate Institute. As was the custom in those years, the private and church-connected institutions of higher learning were largely the initiators of change, with public institutions tending to follow in their wake. Desegregation was a case in point, as private institutions assumed the initiative in this matter. Many years were to pass before public higher education would be pressed into giving the matter its attention.

Public Institutions and Early Court Decisions

The public college has not had the freedom of action often accorded to the private institution. The privileged circumstances of Berea College from 1890 to 1904 in regard to the Kentucky Constitution illustrates that consideration. The southern public colleges, by the familiar 1896 U. S. Supreme Court pronouncement (Plessy vs. Ferguson) of the "separate but equal doctrine," coupled with the tradition of segregation throughout the South, were virtually denied the option of change for more than a generation in the twentieth century.

Early in the 1930's, the restive days of the "New Deal," the National Association for the Advancement of Colored People developed a blueprint for a legal revolution against ethnic discrimination in public education. The university level was selected as the proper point of initial focus, since virtually no provision had been made for the education of Negroes in any of the southern states in graduate and professional fields.[4]

The NAACP. campaign in the courts began with the Hocutt case in North Carolina in 1933, concerning an application to the Law School of the University of North Carolina. The suit was lost on technical grounds. The president of the Negro college attended by the student, Hocutt, refused to certify the plaintiff's scholastic record.[5]

The University of Maryland *v.* Murray case followed soon thereafter, in 1935. Donald Murray's suit was successful, and he was admitted to the Law School of the University of Maryland by the State Court of Appeals. Further South, however, in Virginia and in Tennessee, similar efforts were unsuccessful.[6]

The first test case to reach the U. S. Supreme Court (1935-38) was that of the Gaines *v.* Canada ruling (University of Missouri) in the plaintiff's favor on the grounds that no equal law school for Negroes was then available within the State of Missouri. Proffered aid to attend a Negro law school in a neighboring state was declined by the plaintiff. Soon after the court's ruling, however, a tragedy shrouded in mystery altered the course of history. Gaines, who had established an excellent undergraduate scholastic record and appeared to be a promising law school candidate, disappeared. The circumstances of his disappearance, whether of his own volition or due to foul play, have never been established.[7]

The historic sequel to this event, however, was that no Negro attended a predominantly white institution of higher learning in Missouri for another fifteen years. The grip of tradition held firm until after another world war was fought and won. To what extent the unsolved mystery of Mr. Gaines' disappearance served as a deterrent to desegregation, one can only conjecture.

The crucial court decisions in the historic chain of desegregation events proved to be those against the University of Oklahoma (McLaurin *v.* Oklahoma State Regents for Higher Education) and against the University of Texas (Sweatt *v.* Painter, *et al.*). As Professor Guy B. Johnson expressed it, "those were the cases (1948-50) that cracked the state universities and led to the admission of Negroes to truly southern institutions for the first time."[8]

The first Negro to be admitted to the University of Oklahoma was not a militant young man, not a prototype for the more recent Student Non-Violent Coordinating Committee. He was Mr. G. W. McLaurin, a fifty-four year old retired professor from Langston University seeking to earn a doctorate in the University of Oklahoma's Graduate School of Education. In September 1948, the Federal District Court held Oklahoma's statutes denying him admission to be unconstitutional. He was admitted to the university the following month.

With this desegregation followed what, in retrospect, appears to be appalling segregation. Professor McLaurin was seated in an anteroom adjacent to the classroom so that he could "listen in" during a

lecture. Later permitted to sit in the same classroom, a rail marked
"for colored only" separated him from his classmates. Assigned a
special table in the cafeteria, he ate at a different time from that of other
students. He was a desegregated "untouchable" in a conflict between
laws and the traditional culture.[9]

It is easy to censure the university administration for permitting
these harsh measures, but it is not altogether fair to do so. Oklahoma
statutes required such segregation, and when the plaintiff appealed this
condition of *de facto* resegregation, the Federal District Court denied
his request for relief. The university administration had no legal option.
Two years later, in 1950, the U. S. Supreme Court granted relief from
these deprivations of unequal treatment. All such practices were
promptly discontinued throughout the university without incident.[10]

In many respects, 1948 was a period of ancient history. Many
southern liberals were yet struggling with the concept of how to achieve
a *bona fide* equality and separateness, not a desegregated equality. The
notion of desegregation ran against the grain of cultural conditioning.
R. B. Fosdick expressed the view well, in a different context, with an
empathy that stretches across a generation:

> . . . We cannot go back and rearrange the ideas of an earlier generation
> to make them square with our conceptions today. The most we can do
> is to try to understand the framework within which the pioneers of that
> era carried on their tasks.[11]

And as we climb over the past to the present in our study of the desegregation era, this concept of varying frameworks within which we think
and feel and act will serve us well. It is equally germane to our getting
an insight into the present to remember that, in a cultural sense, it is
not yet 1966 in every nook and cranny of America.

Cracks in the Cake

The resistance to segregation began to weaken during the period
1948–53. Reactions to the incipient stages of desegregation varied
considerably.

In 1953, Professor Guy Johnson, or some member of his staff,
visited each of the then desegregated public colleges and universities
in the South in connection with the Harry Ashmore Project on *The
Negro and the Schools*. The visits revealed a considerable diversity in the
acceptance of desegregation. In Norman, Oklahoma ("The University"), indifference appeared to prevail. In Stillwater, Oklahoma (the
University of Agriculture and Applied Science), however, one Negro
student became a favorite of white students. Several other Negro
students were embarrassed, feeling self-conscious due to the well-inten-

tioned whites going "out of their way to be nice." In Fayetteville, Arkansas (the University of Arkansas), there were no incidents or clashes, but "social interaction" was reported to be at a minimum. Whether the social distance was horizontal or vertical, or both, it was distinctly present. A random sample poll of students five years earlier, in 1948, had shown 68% of the students to favor academic desegregation, but most students opposed desegregation in such social activities as eating together or sharing rooms.

This same ambiguity or ambivalence was shown at the University of Texas where the prevailing feeling was that "the time for social mixing has not yet arrived." (This presumably meant social dancing, because desegregated professional and honor societies, as well as occasional picnics, were not uncommon.) White students arranged a dance and invited the Negro students, who declined the invitation, defining the invitation as a polite but insincere gesture. The white students had earlier agreed that if the Negroes accepted the invitation, they would need to cancel the dance to avoid external pressures and embarrassment to the institution. At Louisiana State University at Baton Rouge, social separateness was maintained, but most students were "nice" to Negroes rather than grumbling or precipitating unpleasant incidents. There was a kind of institutional personality, or a community subculture, that made the collective expectation for behavior markedly different from one university to another.[12]

In 1952, the desegregated southern college was a rarity, but it existed, in both public and private spheres. Private colleges have been sharply criticized for not taking the lead in desegregation, but the fact is that an approximately equal number of private and public institutions in the South were desegregated in 1952. Their desegregation, furthermore, was on a voluntary basis, while virtually every instance of public college desegregation resulted from judicial coercion. Critical generalizations are unsupported by the facts. Church-connected and other non-public institutions did and do range from the liberal to the staunchly conservative, for many varied reasons.

Twenty-one public institutions were listed by *The Negro Year Book* in 1952 as having been previously all white institutions which had by that time admitted Negro students. Paducah Junior College (Kentucky) should be added to that list.[13] Sixteen of these institutions were state colleges or municipal univeristies; two were junior colleges; one was a medical college; another was an A & M college; and two were institutes. The state-by-state distribution of desegregated southern colleges in 1953 shows the hairline cracks in the long-standing tradition of segregation in higher learning. These institutions were the "charter members" of the desegregation era in public higher education. They had their private, voluntary counter-parts as the following table shows:

DESEGREGATED INSTITUTIONS: 1953[14]

	Public	Non public		Public	Non public
Arkansas	1	0	North Carolina ...	1	0
Delaware	1	0	Oklahoma	2	0
Georgie	0	1	Tennessee	1	0
Kentucky	3	6	Texas	2	5
Louisiana	1	1	Virginia...........	5	0
Maryland......	2	3	West Virginia	1	1
Missouri	2	7	District of		
			Columbia	0	3
			TOTAL	22	27

In all public institutions, not more than a thousand Negro students were enrolled in previously all white institutions. Two hundred Negro students were enrolled in the University of Arkansas alone.[15] Mississippi, Alabama, Georgia, Florida, and South Carolina had not yet permitted the enrollment of a Negro student in a public historically all-white institution, nor did they yet show any intention of doing so. The federal courts had made virtually clear, prior to 1954, that public higher education was not to remain segregated, but this did not mean the ultimate decision would not be challenged and circumvented.

The Political Climate (1948–53)

History leaves little doubt that racism, in one form or another, has been a dominant theme in the one-party South for more than a century. The definitive study of V. O. Key, Jr., and his assistant Alexander Heard, *Southern Politics in State and Nation*, provided, in 1949, a perceptive and generally unchallenged documentation on that point. Key discovered that the whites of the "black belt"[16] gave the South its dominant political tone, and that the character of politics of individual states varied roughly with the Negro proportion of the population.[17] On the gubernatorial level, the historical recipe for success, with notable exceptions, consistently included the ingredient frequently referred to as "race baiting." Theodore Bilbo and James K. Vardaman were early masters of that dubious art. Huey P. Long and Ellis Arnall proved exceptions to it.

Key's analysis of the nature and effects of politics within the South stands corroborated by events subsequent to that study, but there is an often overlooked dimension of it. That is the fact that the monolithic South was and continues to be something of a myth. It has not always even been a "one-party South."[18] This position is convincingly developed and explained by such political scientists as Dewey Grantham.[19]

Political stratagems have been understandably ambiguous. The rise and demise of the Dixiecrats in 1948 proved to be the symbol of an outworn political custom, but it was not until 1964 that this fact was recognized with certainty among those who most cherished its memory. The political posture in the South, as the desegregation era began in higher education in the 1940's, was to doubt its authenticity and question its mounting force. How could a recipe that had spelled political success for so long suddenly result in failure? It simply didn't "stand to reason."

As political leaders within the South grappled with their problems, the Southern Governors' Conference was formed to pool judgments and to facilitate collective action in the regional and the national interest. One of the most far-reaching accomplishments of the Governors' Conference was the establishment, in 1949, of the Southern Regional Education Board, charged with the responsibility of attempting to fathom some of the future potential of southern higher education, and with the knowledge and vision thus acquired to stimulate cooperative effort toward useful social and educational ends.

Southern political leaders faced an unprecedented quandary in the matter of desegregation in higher education. The scene shifted to the elementary and secondary school level, and the issue became massive, with the decision of the U. S. Supreme Court in 1954 (Brown v. Board of Education of Topeka), which declared involuntarily segregated public education on all levels to be inherently unequal. The colleges were not suddenly exempt from responsibility to desegregate; they were simply out of the unwelcome spotlight.

Aside from career ambitions, politicians were swayed by numerous considerations in fixing their strategy and tactics. One was the honest personal conviction that segregation was right, a belief that immediately precipitated a division between private and federal loyalty. There were other dilemmas, too. How must, and how may customs change with a minimum of personal and social hurt; how can citizens be urged to accommodate themselves to a new way of life, externally imposed—a way of life which was an immoral accommodation in a sociologically authentic sense?

The Work of Regional Organizations (1948–54)

During the late 1940's and early 1950's, the issues relating to desegregation and to extended opportunities for Negroes in a segregated context mounted rapidly. In the private sphere, more than twenty-five previously white institutions of higher learning had adopted a policy of desegregation prior to 1954. More than a score of public institutions had done so. While nearly all public institutions had become desegregated in compliance with court orders, many students, faculty, and administrators had welcomed, privately or publicly, such orders, accepting them more as enabling than coercive in character.

During those years, a number of regional organizations, working somewhat independently of each other, were furthering the cause of extended educational, economic, and social opportunities for Negroes in segregated and desegregated contexts. Some focused directly on the cause of desegregation. Others considered opportunities for Negroes in the perspective of higher education generally, mindful of many limitations as well as extended opportunities likely to attend desegregation. Other regional groups put the democratic concept to a crucial test in a reconciliation of fundamental differences.

The Southern Education Foundation is the only remaining foundation lineage which, since 1867, has aided the South in its efforts to improve the schools, to raise its living standards, and through education, to get a vision of its integral relationship to the nation and to the world. Pragmatic and patient, it has placed its faith mainly in achieving its goals through raising the levels of understanding, of aspiration, and of competence of Negro southerners. With regular assistance from the General Education Board, the Southern Education Foundation has presumed to serve within the changing culture of which it has been a part, not to pressure social change, but rather to work along the road of education. Theirs has been a long-view strategy, a kind of doctrine of limited goals.

During the period 1948–54, the budget of the Foundation approached $1,000,000, nearly a fifth of that amount coming from the General Education Board.[20] A goodly portion of this budget supported the continuing preparation and service of Negro supervisors (Jeanes Supervisors) begun by the Jeanes Fund in 1908, and continued with support from various other sources over the years. Beginning with the 1950's, the Foundation began to extend and diversify its program. In 1952–53, its program included grants-in-aid for the training of supervisors and principals of public schools for Negroes and for faculty personnel of Negro colleges in the South.[21] As the desegregation era unfolded in subsequent years, the significance of this acute perception in developing *a nucleus of competent Negro leadership in the South* reveals itself to be a kind of readiness program for desegregation in educational

leadership roles. The Foundation did not work overtly for desegregation, but through its efforts helped it to achieve a much larger measure
of success. Its concentration of support to Negro education lessened the
disparity of racial inequality of opportunity wherever its influence was
felt.

The Southern Regional Council, on the other hand, historically
placed central stress on desegregation as a key to opportunity in the
fields of education and other important aspects of society. Not concerned primarily with higher education, the Council was organized from
an earlier interracial council in 1944, and predicated much of its activity
on the conviction that segregation itself had to give way before other
social and educational problems could be grappled with on even terms.
Twenty years prior to the creation of the Equal Opportunity Program
of the U. S. Office of Education, the Council's declared central purpose
was to help achieve "Equal opportunity for all peoples in the South."
Viewing societal desegregation as a necessary antecedent to equal
opportunity and to further social progress, the Council worked publicly
toward that end. In those years the role was a highly unpopular one.
Many of the Council's private supporters preferred to remain anony-
mous, to avoid ostracism and physical jeopardy. The southern white
moderate himself, in 1948–54, was a long way from being free. Meanwhile, the Council, with its research and reportorial activities, provided
a service of making investigations and assembling factual data in
furtherance of the cause of desegregation in lower and higher education,
and within the other social institutions throughout the South.

The Southern Regional Education Board, as previously mentioned,
was founded by the Southern Governors' Conference in 1949 in the
interest of development in higher education for all college capable youth.
The Southern Governors' Conference had advocated a regional plan of
segregated institutions, a plan to which Negro educators were then
publicly opposed.[22] The Board created by it was, in substance, to leave
the issue of desegregation alone, and to follow a policy which recognized
that each state and each institution must make decisions pursuant to
state and federal laws and court decisions.

The selection of educators of integrity strengthened the steadfast-
ness of this purpose. The working position of the Board was described
in a letter in January, 1949, from its first director, Dr. John E. Ivey, Jr.:

> We are trying to develop the program of regional planning for higher
> education so that the issue of segregation. . .is not confused with the
> larger merit of such an educational program. At the same time. . .we
> want to do nothing to discourage them [Negroes] from securing their
> legal rights as defined in the Gaines decision.[23]

In those years of deep travail, the Board managed to steer a difficult true course, working within the broad spectrum of higher education and shifting its foci of attention in tune with emerging social and political realities. It is a tribute to the Southern Governors' Conference that no effort was made to manipulate the Board to digress from its educational charge to serve narrow political ends. The Board kept faith with the educational nature of its purpose, however various governors chose to manage their own intrastate establishments of higher education.

In keeping with the objectives of the Board, the areas of greatest professional need in the South were identified, and financial scholarships were provided to enable students to attend selected public and nonpublic institutions. Medicine, dentistry, and veterinary medicine were identified as the most crucial areas requiring initial cooperative action. Tulane University and Meharry Medical School were among the institutions selected for medical education. Emory University, a church-related institution, was in the selected group in the area of dentistry. The University of Georgia and the University of Oklahoma, along with Tuskegee Institute and the Alabama Polytechnic Institute (now Auburn University) were designated as regional centers for veterinary medicine. Although the latter two institutions are only a few miles apart, they were both retained and strengthened. These were educational plans within what were then considered the prevalent social realities.[24]

The Southern Association of Colleges and Secondary Schools faced a distinctly different set of educational tasks and of social-political dilemmas. Here was the meeting ground of educators (white educators, in a strictly authentic sense) whose views varied widely on the issue of desegregation. In 1948, the Southern Association, consisting of institutional memberships only, did not admit Negro colleges and universities into its membership. A separate organization, "The Association of Colleges and Secondary Schools," was a parallel membership organization for Negroes, consistent with the dual organizational pattern prevalent in the South. The Southern Association, however, did provide "approved listings" of Negro institutions, and many white educators worked actively and cooperatively, making committee visitations to the campuses of Negro institutions in this accreditation activity.

There was no pretense at uniformity of standards among white and Negro institutions; yet standards, as firm as could be reasonably expected, were applicable. As a former Executive Secretary of the Commission on Colleges of the Southern Association expressed it, the Association "did not apply the same rigorous standards" to the Negro

institutions as it did to the white ones.[25] The degree of rigor in accreditation standards is another matter for consideration at another time.[26]
The main points here are that a segregated pattern existed in keeping
with tradition, and that a dual level of standards prevailed in conformity with that same tradition.

The Southern Association was beginning, however, to help the desegregation era to move forward. In 1950, a special committee of the
Southern Association met on two occasions to consider the unsatis-
factory arrangement concerning the dual pattern of accreditation, on
both higher and secondary levels. On the first of these occasions they
met with a comparable group of Negro associates from the Association
of Colleges and Secondary Schools, including such individuals as President Rufus Clement of Atlanta University, President A. W. Dent of
Dillard University (New Orleans), President Felton Clark of Southern
University (Baton Rouge), President A. D. Beitel of Talladega College
(Alabama), and President L. S. Cozard of Barber-Scotia College (North
Carolina). The Southern Association representatives, soon thereafter,
recommended to the parent body—the Association—that "full membership be considered at once for Negro schools."[27]

That recommendation was not then approved. Hardly anyone
thought that it would be, but major steps in the direction of a unified
organization were taken. A standing liaison committee was appointed
to serve the separate associations. Agreement was reached that the
Associations would henceforth meet in the same city on the same dates,
and would avail themselves of the same speakers and consultants when
appropriate. The committee providing the impetus for these changes,
including members of the long-esteemed Highsmith Committee (which
had worked for many years in behalf of articulation between the
Associations), consisted of President Doak S. Campbell of the Florida
State University, Chancellor Harmon Caldwell of the University System
of Georgia, President Ralph Draughon of Auburn University (A. P. I.),
and several others.[28]

Growing out of these and other developments, the Association's
Commission on Colleges and Universities laid out what, in that day,
was a bold blueprint for progress. The design called for on-site committee visitations to all the Negro colleges and universities within the
eleven states of the Association, to assess the strengths, weaknesses,
and needs of these institutions for educational adequacy. Financial
assistance was required for the implementation of the plan, and a grant
from the General Education Board, in the amount of $45,000, was made
to support these visitations. Dr. Hugh McEniry, who worked so closely
with the program through those years, later described the situation:

"As the visitation program neared completion, many hours were whiled away in talk, discussion, and debate as to what to do next. No one seriously thought that the Association would simply continue the approved lists, but no one had an easy answer about next steps either."[29]

Retrospect and Expectation

The few years from 1948 to 1954 marked the active beginning of substantial desegregation in southern higher education. Many changes favorable for ushering in the era were apparent, but they did not just happen. They grew out of individual commitments and collective action, and out of the ability to reach compromise, perhaps on occasion at too dear a price. Nearly fifty previously white institutions were desegregated. With these changes, none the less, there remained a prevailing, puzzling hesitancy about next steps. That hesitancy would be brushed away by the Supreme Court decision of May 17, 1954. That decision would influence a major turn of events in southern higher education. And the whole nation would, in time, become empathically aware that segregation, in higher education or anywhere else, was not uniquely a southern phenomenon.[30] The spotlight of American attention in 1954 was upon the South and the loudspeakers of non-southern public opinion said, "Shame." With humility, with open and covert defiance, with love and enmity, the South worked on, and higher education faced a new kind of responsibility for social progress.

REFERENCES

1. *Oberlin College Bulletin, 1956–66,* 63:3 (April, 1965), p. 7.
2. *Ibid.* It became, as well, the world's first coeducational institution of higher learning.
3. *Berea College Bulletin 1964–65,* 22:1 (September, 1964), p. 9.
4. Joseph P. Guzman, *Twenty Years of Court Decisions Affecting Higher Education in the South* (Department of Records and Research, Tuskegee Institute, June, 1960), p. 1.
5. *Ibid.* This reluctance may be attributed to social threat, physical intimidation, or negligence. Cause was not proven.
6. *Ibid.* Judicial rulings then seemed to vary with the latitude lines.
7. *Ibid.,* p. 4.
8. Guy B. Johnson, "A Survey of the Admission and Integration of Negro Students into Public Institutions of Higher Learning in the South," (unpublished working paper, Study #5, prepared for use by the Ashmore Project [See Harry Ashmore, *The Negro and the Schools,* 1954]. Available at the Joint University Library, Section of Special Collections, Vanderbilt University, Nashville, Tennessee).

9. Guzman, *op. cit.*, p. 11, and Johnson, *op. cit.*, p. 14.

10. Guzman, *op. cit.*, pp. 11–12.

11. Raymond B. Fosdick, *Adventure in Giving* (New York: Harper and Row, 1962), p. 323.

12. Johnson, *op. cit.*, *passim.* Based upon on-campus interviews by sociologists with college officials, students, and others, under the direction of Dr. Guy B. Johnson. Quotes are excerpts from his reports, with his permission.

13. In 1952, the president of Paducah Junior College received a court order to desegregate the institution. He discontinued social functions of student groups and made physical education courses elective. Two years later, the "life time" of the student body, physical education was again required and social functions were resumed without unpleasant incident. R. G. Matheson, in 1966, was still president.

14. J. B. Guzman (Ed.), *The Negro Year Book, 1952* (New York: Wm. H. Wise and Co., Inc. 1952), pp. 239–242.

15. For the record, Arkansas was the only state of the Old Confederacy to admit Negroes to its university without compulsion. To its full credit, it did so without any suggestion from any court.

16. The black belt is a crescent-shaped geographical area extending from Virginia through Georgia, Alabama, and Mississippi to the border of Arkansas and Tennessee. Characterized by its rich black soil, it was ideal for King Cotton and became heavily populated by Negro field hands in the ante-bellum period.

17. *Southern Politics in State and Nation* (New York: Alfred A. Knopf, Inc., 1949), p. 4.

18. Even in the Civil War, or War Between the States, two Republican counties in Alabama reportedly seceded from that state when it seceded from the Union. Then, of course, there were the votes for Herbert Hoover, or against the Catholic, antiprohibition democrat, Al Smith. Most recently, there were the votes for Republican Goldwater.

19. Dewey Grantham, "Politics Below the Potomac," *Current History,* 35 (November 1958), p. 265 and *The Democratic South* (New York: W. W. Norton Company, 1963). *See also*, Allan P. Sindler, "The Passing of the Solid South," *Duke Alumni Register*, 51:1 (January, 1965) and A. P. Sindler (Ed.), *Change in the Contemporary South* (Durham: Duke University Press, 1963).

20. Southern Education Foundation, Inc., "Preliminary Statements of Executive Director in Annual Budget Dockets" (1958–59 through 1964–65). Multilithed and unnumbered.

21. *Ibid.*

22. Hugh H. Smythe, "The Southern Regional Universities Plan," *The Journal of Higher Education*, XXI: March, 1950, p. 123.

23. *Ibid.*, p. 121. The Gaines decision ruled out the states' legal option of providing "equal" education in another state. Thus the Grant-In-Aid provisions developed by the SREB extended student options for higher education in neighboring states, but did not preclude legal recourse beyond these options.

24. A similar development emerged from the establishment of a School of Law for Negroes at Texas Southern University at Houston. Political leaders could yet believe, from the U. S. Supreme Court Decision in the Sweatt *v.* Painter, *et al.* case, that segregation might, under most favorable conditions, be constitutional. (339 U. S. 629, 1949.)

25. Quoted by Hurley H. Doddy, "The Progress of the Negro in Higher Education," *The Journal of Negro Education*, XXXII:4, pp. 485–92. For a fuller account, see Donald Agnew's chapter, "The Southern Association," Lloyd Blauch (Ed.) *Accreditation in Higher Education* (Washington, D. C.: U. S. Office of Education, 1959).

26. The lack of rigor and of relevance, for all Southern higher education institutions will be developed in the forthcoming publication of this study, *Higher Education in the South*.

27. William H. McEniry, "Educational Progress in the Southern States," an address delivered before the Association of Colleges and Secondary Schools in December, 1961, p. 3. Much of the background information in this area was obtained from this source.

28. *Ibid.*

29. *Ibid.*, p. 4.

30. Negro southerners dispersed themselves across America for graduate studies in the liberal universities of the North and West, but returned to the South to become college professors. Some years ago a study revealed that little Fisk University (Nashville) had more Negro faculty members than all the northern and western universities combined. Harvard had none. Desegregation among students was one thing; faculty desegregation was quite another. Yet, in 1954, segregation was viewed as the "Southern problem."

2. The Opening Door

Public higher education's door to desegregation was already unlocked in 1954, by prior decisions of the United States Supreme Court. That door of access was likewise at least ajar in nearly thirty private and church-connected southern colleges and universities. Yet the mood of the South was one of uncertainty. The options available to institutions were not clearly defined, and the honest convictions of fair-minded men and women were divergent. Some felt that desegregation in higher education approached the supreme good as the next step in educational, social, and economic progress. Others believed that only through deliberate gradualism could desegregation accomplish much. Some were alarmed at the risk of social disorganization in higher education which would attend either sudden or gradual desegregation. Still others were convinced that desegregation would only perform a disservice to the cause of higher education among both Negro and white citizens. Among the men and women of good will, in education and in politics, differences of views were pronounced about both ends and means with reference to desegregation in southern colleges and universities.

In anticipation of the pending U. S. Supreme Court decision of Brown *v.* Board of Education of Topeka, and related decisions considered with it, only two consequences could be reasonably foreseen. One was that the Plessy *v.* Ferguson decision of 1896, which built the legal underpinnings for the separate and equal doctrine, would be reversed; that involuntary segregation in public education would be declared inherently unequal and in violation of the Fourteenth Amendment to the U. S. Constitution.

The other prospect, based upon interpretation of the aforementioned cases of Gaines *v.* Canada in Missouri and of Sweatt *v.* Painter in

Texas, was that if segregation were permitted, measurable inequality would no longer be countenanced. (Some counted on a sustained verdict on the basis of the Tenth "States Rights" Amendment.) Each state would then face extreme financial stress in bringing Negro education up to that for Caucasians in the dual educational system, thereby bringing progress in education for the majority to a tragic standstill. In either case, drastic measures and basic policy decisions would be required as an immediate sequel to the Supreme Court decision. That conclusion was inescapable.

When, on May 17, 1954, the Supreme Court announced its decision against a system of involuntary segregation in public education, the ultimate direction of action was clarified. The focus of national attention was quickly shifted to the lower levels of public education, but higher education was not thereby exempt from its own continuing responsibilities for desegregation. With the unequivocal Brown decision came a shock of disbelief, of sorrow and of joy, of hope and anxiety.[1] That the desegregation of public schools would become a reality was, to many, unthinkable. Some said never.[2] Some said not in a thousand years, which proved an accurate prediction rate for the ensuing decade within the deep South.[3]

In higher education, conditions were vastly different. Within a week after the Brown decision, the Supreme Court further ruled, in a pending desegregation suit against the University of Florida (Hawkins v. Board of Education) that its decision would apply to higher education as well, and remanded that case to a lower court for final consideration.[4] Within the ensuing twelve months the number of public desegregated colleges doubled. Private institutions, while not legally affected by those decisions, almost paralleled that rate of growth.

The ensuing decade marked the height of the desegregation era, and many visible and invisible forces were at work in it. This chapter focuses on those more visible quantitative aspects of that decade, the "statistics of change" in desegregation. Subsequent chapters will consider some of the political and legal actions and the more intangible forces and effects of those years, forces less amenable to quantitative treatment and conventional documentation, but none the less real and significant. A view of the growth of desegregation, in public and non-public institutions, in the deep South and in the border states serves to furnish a context of magnitude, a sense of the size of this extension of access to higher education in the Southern regions. There were few "welcome mats" at the historically white colleges but the doors were at least being unlocked and left ajar.

I. THE STATISTICS OF CHANGE

In the decade following the Brown decision, the statistical story can be simply and rather accurately told, thanks largely to the thorough, painstaking efforts of the staff of the Southern Education Reporting Service and the hundreds of individuals and organizational sources supplying information to them. In the Old Confederacy South, twenty-two predominantly Caucasian[5] public colleges and universities were desegregated in 1954. In the spring of 1964, that number had grown to 102, out of a total 170 such institutions. Not one predominantly Negro public college or university in these states was desegregated in 1954, but in 1964, fifteen of forty-two such institutions were desegregated.

In the border states, which have frequently foretold developments in the deeper South, desegregation had been fully achieved in 1964 in the sphere of public higher education (full desegregation, that is, in the limited sense that all institutions were desegregated in fact or in operational admission policies). The number of predominantly Caucasian desegregated institutions in these states rose from thirty-one to the full total of seventy. The predominantly Negro institutions did not have far to go, since seven of the ten such institutions were already desegregated in 1954. The remaining three predominantly Negro institutions became desegregated soon after the May, 1954, rulings of the Supreme Court.[6]

In 1964, the door of college admissions had opened considerably in the public and private spheres, but it still had a long distance to go. Long before 1964, more and more educators and other citizens were coming to recognize the fact that simply providing collegiate access on a desegregated basis did not solve many problems except those of demonstrable legal rights and of moral obligation. Other germane problems, especially the educational and academic ones, blurred the ethnic issue. That is not yet, however, a part of this story. In 1964, 72% of public southern institutions had become desegregated. A bare majority (51%) of church-connected colleges were then desegregated, and 42% of the private colleges had entered this classification. In total, of 600 colleges and universities in the deep and border South in 1964, 350 were desegregated. The other side of the fact needs stress with equal emphasis, 250 were not.[7]

Voluntary and involuntary action cannot be sharply divided into individual or collective decision-making. Freedom and compulsion are not fully separate. Persons and institutions cannot be sliced apart. Similarly, the terms "independent" and "public" (i.e. dependent on public support) institutions do not represent mutually exclusive distinctions. These points became emphatically clear with the passage of the historic Civil Rights Act of 1964. A major educational provision of that Act, the Assurance of Compliance, was of greater historic moment in both public and nonpublic decisions to desegregate southern institutions of higher education than any other single event since 1954.[8] The sudden rise in the reported number of compliant institutions gives an impression of inflated distortion. This impression is correct to some degree. However, numerous preliminary compliance reviews of colleges and universities as well as elementary and secondary schools have been conducted to assure bona fide compliance. The "Explanation" of that Assurance is reproduced in the appendix of this study.

GRAPH I

DESEGREGATION AMONG PUBLIC, HISTORICALLY CAUCASIAN COLLEGIATE
INSTITUTIONS IN THE ELEVEN OLD CONFEDERACY STATES, 1954–66

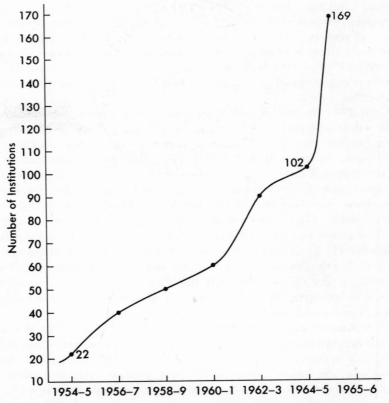

Sources: "Ten Years in Review," *Southern School News* (May 17, 1964), p. 3, and cumulative lists #c-24 of "Colleges and Universities which Have Signed an Assurance of Compliance, up to March 7, 1966.

GRAPH II

DESEGREGATION AMONG 45 PUBLIC, HISTORICALLY NEGRO COLLEGIATE
INSTITUTIONS IN THE ELEVEN OLD CONFEDERACY STATES, 1954–64

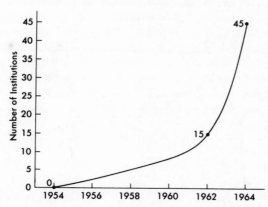

Sources: Ibid.

GRAPH III

DESEGREGATION AMONG PUBLIC, HISTORICALLY CAUCASIAN COLLEGIATE
INSTITUTIONS IN THE BORDER STATES OF DELAWARE, THE DISTRICT OF
COLUMBIA, KENTUCKY, MARYLAND, MISSOURI, OKLAHOMA, AND WEST
VIRGINIA 1954–64

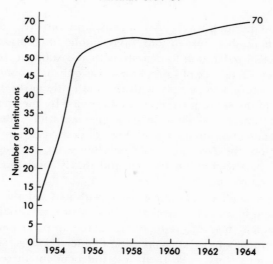

Sources: Ibid.

GRAPH IV

DESEGREGATION AMONG PUBLIC, HISTORICALLY NEGRO COLLEGIATE INSTITUTIONS IN THE BORDER STATES OF DELAWARE, THE DISTRICT OF COLUMBIA, KENTUCKY, MARYLAND, MISSOURI, OKLAHOMA, AND WEST VIRGINIA

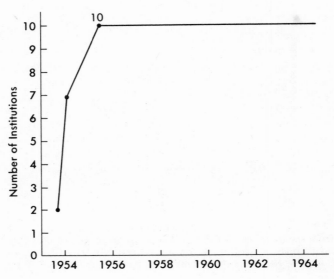

Sources: Ibid.

There was nothing in the Act legally and directly coercive with reference to nonpublic institutions, and public institutions were already under legal obligation to comply with the substantive provisions of the Act. The Assurance of Compliance was only a "voluntary" agreement of an institution to comply with the sixth title of the Civil Rights Act of 1964 and the subsequent regulations issued by the Department of Health, Education and Welfare in its implementation. Because of its crucial significance in "finalizing" the era of desegregation in southern higher education, the Assurance of Compliance form is reproduced in full below. It has been much revered and much condemned, but it is none the less significant.

Its intent and effect, of course, is to withhold federal funds, massively increasing in amounts, availability, and variety of purposes, from institutions which choose to remain segregated and independent. The federal government's indirect, increasing financial sponsorships of nonpublic institutions thus make them less independent in some respects than they have ever been before.

ASSURANCE OF COMPLIANCE WITH THE DEPARTMENT OF HEALTH, EDUCATION, AND WELFARE REGULATION UNDER TITLE VI OF THE CIVIL RIGHTS ACT OF 1964

_____ (hereinafter called the "Applicant")
(Name of Applicant)

HEREBY AGREES THAT it will comply with title VI of the Civil Rights Act of 1964 (P.L. 88-352) and all requirements imposed by or pursuant to the Regulation of the Department of Health, Education, and Welfare (45 CFR Part 80) issued pursuant to that title, to the end that, in accordance with title VI of that Act and the Regulation, no person in the United States shall, on the ground of race, color, or national origin, be excluded from participation in, be denied the benefits of, or be otherwise subjected to discrimination under any program or activity for which the Applicant receives Federal financial assistance from the Department; and HEREBY GIVES ASSURANCE THAT it will immediately take any measures necessary to effectuate this agreement.

If any real property or structure thereon is provided or improved with the aid of Federal financial assistance extended to the Applicant by the Department, this assurance shall obligate the Applicant, or in the case of any transfer of such property, any transferee, for the period during which the real property or structure is used for a purpose for which the Federal financial assitance is extended or for another purpose involving the provision of similar services or benefits. If any personal property is so provided, this assurance shall obligate the Applicant for the period during which it retains ownership or possession of the property. In all other cases, this assurance shall obligate the Applicant for the period during which the Federal financial assistance is extended to it by the Department.

THIS ASSURANCE is given in consideration of and for the purpose of obtaining any and all Federal grants, loans, contracts, property, discounts or other Federal financial assistance extended after the date hereof to the Applicant by the Department, including installment payments after such date on account of applications for Federal financial assistance which were approved before such date. The Applicant recognizes and agrees that such Federal financial assitance will be extended in reliance on the representations and agreements made in this assurance, and that the United States shall have the right to seek judicial enforcement of this assurance. This assurance is binding on the Applicant, its successors, transferees, and assignees, and the person or persons whose signatures appear below are authorized to sign this assurance on behalf of the Applicant.

Dated _____   _____
                                              (Applicant)

                                    By _____
                                        (President, Chairman of Board, or comparable
                                                authorized official)

_____

(Applicant's mailing address)

HEW-441
(12-64)

   In January, 1966, the desegregation era in southern higher education, in its conventionally used sense, was near its end. The remaining segregated institutions unwilling to sign assurances of compliance
were few indeed. The question of desegregated access had been virtually
resolved. Here is the account of the compliance assurances during the
phasing-out period of segregation in southern higher education, 1964–
65.[9]

TABLE I
TOTAL INSTITUTIONS DESEGREGATED IN JANUARY 1966

State	Desegregated Institutions	State	Desegregated Institutions
Alabama	42	Mississippi	36
Arkansas	21	North Carolina	86
Florida	65	South Carolina........	31
Georgia	53	Tennessee	53
Kentucky	40	Texas	119
Louisiana	22	Virginia	44
		Total	612

   The report of compliance assurances is difficult to interpret accurately for two reasons. First of all, it does not consist of a comparable
group of institutions of higher learning, including as it does, a number of
academies, nonaccredited institutions, and some "colleges" not listed in
the *Education Directory* of the Office of Education, commonly used for
comparative purposes. Secondly, the genuine intent to comply cannot
always be adduced without supporting information about the institutional signatories and the community milieu of individual institutions.
With these disclaimers, the following graph provides a single total
time-line of calculated desegregation in the South from which a com-
posite picture can be developed.

GRAPH V
THE TIME LINE OF DESEGREGATION IN
SOUTHERN HIGHER EDUCATION, 1948–66
in 513 Public and Nonpublic Institutions

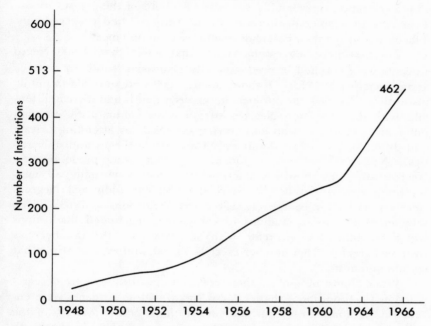

Sources: Southern Education Reporting Service, especially, News Release of October 8, 1964; *Southern School News*, May, 1964, and May, 1965. Unofficial sources from church and private groups, U. S. Office of Education and other agencies. Eleven deep South states, including Arkansas and excluding Kentucky, 214 public institutions, and 299 private institutions are included in this estimate. Data gathered from such diverse sources cannot be precisely accurate, but in the main they tell the truth.

✐ The *de facto* desegregation of an institution obviously does not approximate a reliable index of the desegregated character of its enrollment. An institution with one student from an ethnic minority is technically desegregated as truly as is one with hundreds of students from the Negro or non-Negro population.✐ It has achieved the non-zero condition. It is important to get an indication of what has been called "tokenism" in the sense of actual enrollment figures through the years.[10] Full token desegregation, of course, could be accomplished with only a few hundred Negro students. In explicit terms, the number of Negroes enrolled in predominantly Caucasian southern institutions in 1952 would have been more than ample—uniformly distributed—to have achieved full institutional desegregation at that time throughout the South. To give institutional examples of the limitations of desegregation compliance, the University of Mississippi—with four Negro students—would be as desegregated as Southern Illinois University with an uncounted number of Negro students of more than four hundred.[11] Campus observations in 1965 showed considerable out-of-class segregation, presumably voluntary, in both of these institutions. Then, of course, some institutions which "comply" find it exceedingly difficult in proving their bona fide assurance of compliance.[12]

The best informed estimates are that fewer than 1,500 Negro students were enrolled in predominantly Caucasian southern colleges and universities in 1953. Of those, about 1,000 were enrolled in public institutions. In 1964, the numbers in the deep South had increased tenfold, with 10,000 or more Negroes attending predominantly Caucasian public institutions, and an additional 5,000 Negroes attending private and church-connected predominantly Caucasian colleges and universities. Nearly 25,000 Negro students were attending predominantly Negro institutions in which a few white students, virtually all non-southerners, were enrolled.[13] More than 50,000 additional Negroes were yet enrolled in completely segregated institutions in 1965.[14] The number of Caucasian students in completely segregated institutions would be difficult to estimate with accuracy, but the number has dwindled greatly. That number exceeds 30,000, and may be triple that certain minimum.

While almost 60% of southern collegiate institutions were desegregated in 1964, not more than 15% of Negro college students were enrolled in predominantly Caucasian institutions. *Fewer than 2%* of the million students in predominantly Caucasian institutions in the South were Negroes compared with about 10% of the total population figures.[15]

II. WHAT DIFFERENCE DOES IT MAKE?

We have viewed in quantitative terms the desegregation movement in southern higher education. The bodily quantity of change, of course, raises questions about the net qualitative effects of this development, with its uprooting ironies as well as its evident benefits. From the standpoint of the dire predictions of tragedy and violence, the historic fact is reassuring that with this accelerated social evolution there have been incidents of serious disorder only on the campuses of three state universities, while more than 500 institutions have now achieved some degree of *de facto* desegregation.

This fact is due in part to the prevailing conciliatory political leadership within the southern states when crucial decisions could no longer be temporized or postponed. The political dimension of the "showdown" cases at the University of Mississippi, the University of Alabama, and the University of Georgia, despite their attending violence, are yet of particular significance because they announced to the nation unmistakably that there would be no turning back to the pre-1954 era of segregation in higher education. The 15,000 Negro students in historically Caucasian institutions in 1964 have been of inestimable significance; coupled with those thousands of students, the crucial test cases of admission of fewer than a dozen or so Negro students have made continuing admissions throughout the South emphatically secure. A statistic of one or two, if it is Harvey Gantt at Clemson University, or James Meredith at Ole Miss, or Charlayne Hunter and Hamilton Holmes at the University of Georgia, is of far greater societal significance than that of the first hundred students who follow in the paths they have cleared. However important the statistics of change, the full depth of meaning derives from the roots out of which these changes grow. These have been largely the roots of law and of politics.

REFERENCES

1. The White Citizens Council called it Black Monday. Thurgood Marshall, then chief legal advisor of the National Association for the Advancement of Colored People, began talking of a new civil rights calendar in terms of it, BSCD and ASCD (Supreme Court Decision).
2. In 1966 the (white) Citizens (Council) Private School Association continued to be actively engaged in establishing new segregated private schools in Southern states. Their support is languishing.
3. In the eleven states of the Old Confederacy, only 1.18% of Negro pupils, in May 1964, were enrolled in previously all-white public schools. *Southern School News*, Nashville: Southern Education Reporting Service 10:11 (May 1964), p. 1.
4. "Ten Years in Review," *Southern School News* (Nashville: Southern Education Reporting Service, May 17, 1964), p. 3.
5. The author begs the reader's occasional indulgence, for the sake of accuracy, in the use of this term. Caucasian is to Negro as black is to white. To use "Negro" and "white" seems inaccurate.
6. The border states here refer to Missouri, Maryland, West Virginia, Delaware, Kentucky, Oklahoma, and the District of Columbia.
7. Guy B. Johnson, "Desegregation in Southern Higher Education," *Higher Education* XX:9 (June 1964), p. 5.
8. In January 1966, all public institutions of higher learning in the

South except one junior college in Scooba, Mississippi, had "signed the pledge." Nearly all nonpublic colleges had likewise "complied."

9. Based upon a list of colleges and universities which have signed an Assurance of Compliance form issued by the Director, Equal Education Opportunities Program, U. S. Office of Education. Dated, August 6, 1965, November 11, 1965 with additions to January 7, 1966. Such assurances were not perfunctory, and challenged instances were subject to whatever investigations seemed warranted by the federal government. In 1965, none had been rejected by the U. S. Office of Education.

   For fuller information on compliance the reader is referred to "Title 45-Public Welfare," *Federal Register*, December 4, 1964.

10. "Tokenism" has developed an unfortunate connotation. For one institution to admit a single student from an ethnic minority has been a signal achievement. For another to admit scores of such students has been accomplished with only token effort. Dr. Henry Hill, President Emeritus of George Peabody College for Teachers, puts it this way: "It is a good symptom when a college recruits and admits a few well-qualified Negro students. It is not a good symptom when it admits a group of Negroes wholesale who are not qualified." (Notes on prepublication manuscript, January 10, 1966.)

11. With the well-intentioned, but possibly misguided notion that no identifiable records of race be maintained, we will only be able to estimate the extent and qualitative effect that desegregation is having in higher education unless this policy is reversed. Once we can safely assume that information will be put more to constructive than injurious use, perhaps policy can be modified to fit new realities. A recent step has been taken in that direction with spot census taking by race, but with no permanent individual identification.

12. Grambling College, in Louisiana, for example, would find it difficult to recruit Caucasian students, even though they would be welcomed within the institutional culture. The coach is especially anxious to desegregate his football squad with first-rate athletes. Likewise, Georgia Southwestern College, a signatory of the Assurance of Compliance, would find recruitment of Negro students exceedingly difficult in view of the recent racial violence in Americus and the ostracism of one of its leading citizens who sought to establish lines of biracial communication.

13. According to a recent survey, among the forty-eight predominantly Negro institutions which are desegregated, thirty-four enrolled not more than five non-Negro students. Earl McGrath, *The Predomi-*

nantly Negro Colleges and Universities in Transition (New York: Teachers College Press, 1965), p. 15.

14. Johnson, op. cit., p. 6.

15. This does not mean that 10% of the population of college students are Negroes, but only that 10% of the college-age population are. The problem of helping Negro students qualify for and get a chance to go to college is a far greater problem, from the standpoint of numbers, than the imbalanced ratio in desegregation terms.

3. Politics and the Law

The statistics of the desegregation era have conveyed some measure of its progress, both on an institutional and student enrollment basis. To know those statistics, as we are all aware, does not assure any real understanding of what caused them. They are governed, in the main, either by or through political leadership—in church and state. The turning point of history in the era of desegregation generally, and in public higher education particularly, may well have resided in the resolution of crises, state by state, at the level of gubernatorial decision.

The brief period of this era, as man measures time, cannot be accurately portrayed without attention to its socio-political aspects and to the concurrent legislation regulating public and nonpublic higher education, a distinction that is becoming increasingly blurred in both legal and in functional terms. The law, as well as the political context in which it functions or malfunctions, has been of central significance in these years. It explains much of what we have already witnessed, and further helps us to anticipate much of what yet awaits us.

I. THE GOVERNOR'S ROLE IN THE DESEGREGATION ERA

As former Governor Sanford, of North Carolina, commented at the 1965 White House Conference on Education, education is in politics, belongs there, and is bound to stay there. The task is to employ political influence in the educational interest. In the tortuous, agonizing road toward desegregation, state and church, and private politics have all been present on each step of the journey, helping...and hurting. Through it all, the onus of unpopular decisions has been upon the courts, but they have at least been insulated to a degree by some immunities from popular protests. The southern governor, faced with the impasse of court decisions versus his electorate, has stood in visible isolation—an open target for all special interest groups.

The dilemma of politicians, directly responsible to the electorate, was aptly phrased by Theodore White to the effect that they "must devote as much of their time looking backward," to make sure they are being followed, "as looking forward to find where they should go."[1]

A definitive investigation of the governor's role in connection with desegregation in higher education was conducted for the Southern Higher Education Study by the political scientist, R. E. Cleary. In attempting to get a representative cross section of the South, while recognizing that there really isn't one, he selected the states of North Carolina, Georgia, and Mississippi for three intensive case studies. His study was aided by published reports concerning relevant events in each of these states.[2] Cleary's study focused upon the initial cases of admission of Negroes into the respective state universities of these states, the social and political climate in which gubernatorial decisions were made, and the observable consequences of those decisions.

TABLE I
POPULATION ACCORDING TO RACE, 1960

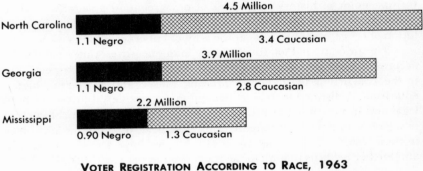

4.5 Million

North Carolina

1.1 Negro   3.4 Caucasian

3.9 Million

Georgia

1.1 Negro   2.8 Caucasian

2.2 Million

Mississippi

0.90 Negro   1.3 Caucasian

VOTER REGISTRATION ACCORDING TO RACE, 1963

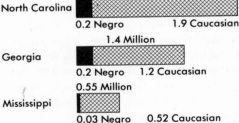

2.1 Million

North Carolina

0.2 Negro   1.9 Caucasian

1.4 Million

Georgia

0.2 Negro   1.2 Caucasian

0.55 Million

Mississippi

0.03 Negro   0.52 Caucasian

Source. U. S. Bureau of Census, Population Figures, decennial census, and Voter Education Project Registration Report. The Department of Commerce estimates 1960–65 increases of 9% in North Carolina, 6 to 7% in Georgia, and 5 to 6% in Mississippi, but no recent estimates by race were available from the Bureau of the Census.

It will be helpful to note the different racial composition of the three states chosen for Cleary's study and the differences in Negro voting registration at that time, shown in Table I, keeping in mind the V. O. Key thesis of the significance of this factor. We must remind ourselves as well of the changing Negro enfranchisement in the South since the "crisis decisions" in those states.

The number of Negro registrants climbed in the eleven former Confederate states, in 1964, to 2,174,000 or 43.3% of the Negroes of voting age.[3] A study by Lloyd Elliot reported that Negro southerners gave President Johnson 1,400,000 votes, consisting of from 43 to 56 electoral college votes.[4] The Voting Rights Act of 1965 changed the picture again. Ten weeks after its passage, 110,000 Negroes registered in the states of Alabama, Georgia, Mississippi, South Carolina, and Louisiana; 29,213 Negroes registered in Mississippi alone.[5] But the gubernatorial crises were not in 1966. Those were in 1956, 1961, and 1962. The political realities and conjectures were far different then as Table I reveals. In 1966, Attorney General Richmond Flowers, gubernatorial aspirant in Alabama, conjectured that, with 20 to 30% of the votes of Caucasian citizens, a substantial support of Negro voters would yield him a majority.

North Carolina

Four Negroes were admitted to the University of North Carolina in 1951 by court order, without incident and with little public attention. In 1954, Governor W. B. Umstead expressed public disappointment regarding the Supreme Court ruling in the Brown case, and asked the University's Institute of Government to study the problems and reasonable options growing out of that decision. Resistance, acquiescence, and token compliance were the alternatives explored. Subsequently, the Pearsall Committee recommended an inch-by-inch resistance, within the laws—an involuntary compliance.

Lt. Governor Luther Hodges became governor in November 1954, upon the death of Governor Umstead. In this new role he avoided taking a strong stand, discouraged publicity, and used every legal means to prevent what he regarded as an erroneous decision of the Supreme Court in 1956 from hampering public education.[6] He was convinced that the people of North Carolina, presumably the voting constituency, would not support the mixing of races in public schools.

He first supported the University trustees in denying admission to Negro applicants, but promptly agreed to their admission upon a federal district court order in 1956. As Cleary explained his posture, "He did nothing to inflame the situation, but attempted to ease it." (The historically Caucasian North Carolina State College at Raleigh had been admitting Negro students to its graduate school for three years, since 1953.) With dignity, social and political sensitivity—and in good conscience—this segregationist opened the way for ultimate desegregation through the orderly process of debate, compromise, and respect for law. Higher education, largely untroubled, moved forward.

Subsequent events have measured the effect of this stratagem of legal resistance, and of acquiescence when legal recourse had reached a true impasse. Governor Hodges saw and pointed to that reality.[7] Governor Terry Sanford used this momentum to press for excellence in lower and higher education, within the context of the law, to meet the needs for education and to comply with desegregation requirements.

Georgia

The political strategy in Georgia came five years later and was of a different order, but it had some of the earmarks of the North Carolina setting. Charlayne Hunter and Hamilton Holmes had both done well in their high school academic studies, and Holmes had achieved a brilliant record. They applied for admission to the University of Georgia in July, 1959. Time passed. A year and a half later, Judge W. A. Bootle ruled that they had been denied admission solely on the basis of race. Governor Ernest Vandiver had succeeded Governor Marvin Griffin, and had matched his inflammatory words: Griffin had said, "Come hell or high water, races will not be mixed in Georgia Schools . . . as long as I am governor."[8] But that was in 1954. Vandiver added: "Not one, no, not one, Negro will go to school [with whites] while I am in office."[9] That was five years later, and that was different. Judge Bootle's verdict forced some gubernatorial action.

Georgia, under the administration of Governor Vandiver, had postponed a showdown in higher education for three years. This had been through adroit maneuvers, but maneuvers were at an end. After conferring with advisers, Governor Vandiver took the case out of the hands of the Board of Regents and assumed full official responsibility for decision-making. In an address to the Georgia legislature, he emphasized that Georgia could not afford to abandon public education. In rapid sequence, he then announced a temporary closing of the University of Georgia and requested the legislature to repeal the legislation which would cut off public funds from any desegregated institution. His action was not in time. This was the final moment of reckoning with the judiciary.

Judge Bootle issued a temporary restraining order preventing Governor Vandiver from closing the University on January 10, 1961, and the following day became " D Day" at the University of Georgia. An aggregation of more than 1,000 irate Caucasian Georgians appeared that evening in front of Miss Hunter's dormitory, Myers Hall, and bricks were thrown into her room. This near riot immediately followed a basketball game between Georgia and its keenest rival, Georgia Tech. Georgia had lost.

Had it not been for the alert, positive action of Mayor Ralph Snow, of Athens, Georgia, "D Day" at the University of Georgia could easily have resulted in a far worse tragedy than Ole Miss was later to experience. Mayor Snow telephoned the Governor who delayed authorizing the use of the State Patrol to control the mob. He deployed the entire Athens police force of forty-one men, who used tear gas to immobilize the mob. The local fire department was called in to turn their hoses on the rioters. He called the Director of the State Department of Public Safety, who said that he was not empowered to order the state troopers into action without permission from the Governor. Mayor Snow then phoned the Governor again, who, after being informed that the Negroes were under suspension, ordered troopers to be sent to Myers Hall.

Cleary's observation is correct to the effect that "Governor Vandiver honored the law and bowed to the inevitable . . . In the final analysis, Vandiver declared that Georgia would uphold the law and order and preserve her educational system, and then he presented a concrete program to achieve these goals."[10] Yet, had it not been for the decisive action of the Mayor of Athens, he might never have had this opportunity. The Mayor deployed every force at his disposal to the cause of law and order while the Governor remained indecisive.

The Governor of Georgia helped to shape its future in yielding to the rulings of the federal government's judicial branch. (Neither Congress nor the executive branch of the federal government had yet taken any action of consequence.) Since that pivotal event in Georgia history, the Regents have not acted in defiance or overt circumvention of any laws, but have moved with honor toward their *bona fide* acceptance.

Mississippi

There is no value in laboring the inhumane tragedy at Ole Miss. Yet the lessons from that event are a necessary part of assembling the jigsaw puzzle of desegregation in southern higher learning.[11] Besides, the prospects for the future, too little publicized, are good. The dormitories vacated in the aftermath of the crisis have been filled again. The Negro students now enrolled there are not harassed as was their predecessor James Meredith. Recent conversations with administrators and faculty members there point to a genuine spirit of compliance with the law in good faith and with good manners devoid of hostility.

The story needs recounting, but we need to remember that 1962 in Mississippi was "longer ago" in this respect than almost anywhere in America. With dignity and deep hurt, Mississippi is surging ahead to rejoin the Union. Governor Paul Johnson reminded his fellow Mississippians, in 1965, that "defiance and loud talking" will not protect the people of that state, that theirs "must not be a rear-guard defense of a century-old past," but that they must claim, for themselves and the welfare of the rising generation, their "share of tomorrow." Rather than be a second Los Angeles, he declared, Mississippi must recognize that law and order are important to all of its citizens.[12]   Every social system depends, for its own survival, upon the maintenance of order and general conformity to the value norms of that system. Changing those value norms without a collapse of lawful compliance was, in Mississippi, a problem with no "school solution."

In 1962, when James H. Meredith attempted to enroll at the University of Mississippi, Governor Ross Barnett's options for circumvention were at an end. He faced the ultimate decision. His predecessors, Governors Hugh White and James P. Coleman[13] had managed to pass this "decision of no return" along to him. When, on September 13, Judge Sidney Mize enjoined University officials (the Chancellor, Registrar, and Board of Trustees) from continuing to refuse to admit Meredith, Governor Barnett announced that:

> No school will be integrated in Mississippi while I am your governor
> . . . every public official, including myself, should be prepared to make
> the choice tonight whether he will submit or whether he is willing to
> go to jail . . . .[14]

The Trustees named Governor Barnett a special registrar, with full power to handle the Meredith case. With this newly vested authority, coupled with his general executive powers as Governor, he personally rejected Mr. Meredith's application for admission. In quick succession, the Justice Department asked the Court of Appeals to cite the Trustees for contempt of its orders; the Court so acted, and the Trustees ordered James Meredith to report to the Board, which promptly agreed to register him.[15]

Governor Barnett continued to be intransigent, and on September 25 issued an executive order directing the state police to arrest and jail any federal officer who attempted to interfere with a state official engaged in the performance of his duties. Despite being enjoined by the circuit court from interfering with the scheduled registration, he walked across the street from the state capitol to the Board of Trustees office, flanked by an entourage of highway patrolmen, blocked the doorway to the suite, and refused Meredith admittance.   The following day, Lt. Governor Paul Johnson, on instructions from the Governor, served to obstruct a repeated registration attempt in a similar manner.[16]

The familiar details subsequent to this climax do not warrant full repetition here.   The Commission on Colleges of the Southern Association of Colleges and Schools notified the Governor of its decision to recommend to the Association a withdrawal of accreditation of every public Mississippi college unless he vacated his political registrar post and restored full authority to the Board of Trustees.   President John Kennedy and Attorney General Robert Kennedy conferred with the Governor by telephone on more than twenty occasions.   He vacillated from the position of lawful compliance to that of lawless defiance.

The pledge that "we will never surrender," the tragic, violent riot, the two deaths, and the pathetic capitulation fourteen minutes after his "never" pledge, that "we must have peace and harmony," were words from a man overwhelmed by the enormity of the problem of which he was a part.   That chapter of history is closed now, and a brighter one has begun.   The native Caucasian citizens of Mississippi were, and are, segregationists, to be sure.   They inherited segregation as truly as they did Protestantism, an agrarian way of life, a fertile delta soil and a beautiful gulf coast.   But they are, in the main, coming to measure up to the collective American expectation.

In 1966, a positive mood is apparent as change has come finally to Mississippi.   Vanquished many of them feel, but unbowed.   If those who regard themselves as the victors can wear their triumph with love and humility rather than a gloating spirit, the future of Mississippi and of desegregated higher education in it may be bright indeed.   If they do not, there will be no victors.

II.   THE FORCE OF CURRENT LAW

The political story of desegregation in southern higher education from 1948 to 1964 was largely one of judicial action and of executive response to it.   The legislative branch of government became central in the rapid evolution of this era in 1964.

The law, especially the judiciary, had formed the yeast of social change among a restive Negro people in the setting of a troubled national conscience.   The non-South until recently had been able to contain or cover its guilt; the South had not.

Since the Civil Rights Act of 1957 and the court decisions on various levels from 1948 to 1964, no segregated college—public or private—has been able to rest in peace.   In legal terms, of course, the pressure has been upon public colleges, and the litigations have covered untold tons of pages of briefs in testing hundreds of laws.[17] The fact was clearly established by 1965 that the day is past for any concept of deliberate speed. Public colleges are required to be desegregated now, including every officially sponsored aspect of collegiate life—from classrooms to cafeterias, from football games to fraternities. While the burden of proof would be difficult and tedious in some delicate areas, a sufficient consensus of precedents now assures the affirmative outcome of any lawsuit pursued to test the principle of practice to its conclusion.[18]

The next question, which used to be easily answered, now becomes an imponderable one. What is a public college? Professor Jerre Williams defines it as one which obtains "substantial, general support from public funds, whether they be local, state, or federal."[19] He points out that a college is not made public by "specifically defined, publicly supported projects." The college is required to prevent racial discrimination regarding such projects, and with reference to administering loaned public funds and the like. These spheres of public support, however, do not make it a public college from the standpoint of college policy unrelated to such projects and public loaned funds. Until 1964, therefore, and even after as shown hereafter, the private college could be a legal sanctuary for segregationists. If a private college could segregate on the basis of sex, geography, or religion, it could—and can—continue to do so on the basis of race alone. That is the cherished freedom accorded a private institution in our American democracy.

But the law is a carrot as well as a stick. It provides positive sanctions as well as negative restraints. The Civil Rights Act of 1964 provided a spectacular example of the financial incentives for desegregation among private institutions. This incentive, in the form of the Title VI Assurance of Compliance, was discussed in the preceding chapter. The $2.6 billion Higher Education Act of 1965, coupled with the Higher Education Facilities Act of 1963, added to the temptation of the carrot. In some cases, it put to the hard test the independence of many of the "independent" institutions of higher learning.

The Civil Rights Act was signed by President Johnson on July 2, 1964. Four of its titles have direct relevance for desegregation in southern higher education, and most pointedly in the context of non-public education, since public education's position of mandatory compliance was no longer in question, in principle or in practice, in 1964.

Title IV made clear that Negro and Caucasian public institutions are to eliminate racial discrimination. A further provision of that title is that colleges and universities (public or nonpublic) may establish

Civil Rights Institutes to facilitate the desegregation process in public schools. Nearly thirty institutions in the South did so during the summer of 1965. More were expected to take an active part thereafter.

Title II prohibits discrimination in the restriction of public accommodations on the basis of race, religion, color, or national origin. In some sectors here again, the nonpublic college is not covered. Dormitories would not be covered by this provision presumably, unless constructed with federal government loans or grants. However, college cafeterias would be covered if patronage by nonstudents in the community were permitted. As Professor Williams explains it, "The law eliminates race or religion as the ground of discrimination as long as you are open to the public. You may validly discriminate on other grounds . . . And, of course, you can discriminate on these grounds so long as there is no trespass into the public sector."[20]

Beyond policy, the matter of personal discrimination is again prevented by law, the burden of proof being on the person claiming a violation of the statute, based upon evidence that discrimination was on a racial or religious basis.

Title VII relates to equal employment opportunity and covers all employers engaged in interstate commerce. This would include any private college with out-of-state students, which in practice means all or virtually all institutions. This provision became effective in July, 1965, and contained an exemption to religious institutions on religious but not on racial grounds, and to the employees of private institutions performing an "educational function."

Title VI, however, is apt to be the longest remembered, because its incentives brought most of the remaining southern colleges and universities around to *de facto* desegregation. The U. S. Office of Education, the federal courts, and the constant surveillance of the National Association for the Advancement of Colored People will be involved in assuring a *bona fide* compliance. No one can expect whole-hearted institutional support for a bought compliance. Title VI bars discrimination in any federally assisted programs, however small the level of that assistance. Yet there is an increasing basis for hope, despite the inauspicious circumstances of Title VI desegregation.

The force of the law has been and continues to be the central factor in desegregation, but it "has gone about as fer as it kin go." Its combined power through restraint by law and through financial support with the desegregation "rider" has made it formidable to segregationists, highly salutary to others. After more than a generation of litigations and new legislation, the substantive questions have been given explicit answers. There is a fixed definition of the musts, the must nots, and the mays. With the options known, the South and the nation can proceed with increased assurance. The new norms are clear in the legal dimensions of our social order.

III. THE MEANING OF THE PRESENT

A young seaman, on his first voyage, looking over the broad expanse of water, remarked to his Chief Petty Officer in amazement, "Gosh! What a lot of ocean!" The Chief replied, with a deliberately casual air, "You don't really see the ocean; all you see is what's on top." Our consideration of the statistics of desegregation through time, and of the politics and the laws governing it, have only provided us with a surface view. It is possible to redouble one's efforts while losing sight of his goal. For some, desegregation itself has been a goal; for others, a means to one; for others, an anathema.

The story of the opening of the collegiate door, and of the legal and political influences in that opening, has been one of cultural turmoil and of much personal travail. We need to view this era in more analytical and contemplative terms, in an effort to wring out of it the secrets of prudence for the present and future. While publicized forces have been at work to achieve desegregation, other forces, largely unpublicized, have worked to give it a depth of meaning far beyond the limited goal of desegregation itself. In the dynamics of that account, we come beyond head counting in desegregation; closer to the heart of its meaning.

REFERENCES

1. Theodore White, *The Making of the President, 1964* (New York: Atheneum Publishers, 1965), p. *x*, foreword.
2. R. E. Cleary, "Gubernatorial Politics and Desegregation in Public Higher Education" (mimeographed; Nashville, Tennessee, 1964). Related published studies will be cited subsequently.
3. Voter Education Project News Release of the Southern Regional Council, Atlanta, Georgia, November 15, 1964.
4. Lloyd J. Elliot, "The Negro Voter and National Politics," *New South*, 20:9 (September, 1965).
5. William J. Taylor (Staff Director), *The Voting Rights Act . . . The First Months* (Washington: The U. S. Commission on Civil Rights, 1965).
6. Cleary, *op. cit.*, p. 14. This ruling, referring specifically to LeRoy B. Frasier, Ralph K. Frasier, and John L. Brandon, established once again the applicability of the Brown case to higher education.
7. See Governor Luther H. Hodges' *Businessman in the Statehouse* (Chapel Hill: University of North Carolina Press, 1962).

8. *Southern School News*, Nashville: Southern Education Reporting Service, October 1, 1954, p. 6.

9. Ernest Vandiver, "State of the State," January 15, 1959 (mimeographed). Also see *Southern School News*, February 1959, p. 10.

10. Cleary, *op. cit.*, p. 24. If the reader is interested in a fuller account, a vivid report from a different point of view, he is referred to the publication by Calvin Trillin, *An Education in Georgia* (New York: The Viking Press, 1963).

11. In addition to the analytical unpublished account of R. E. Cleary, the reader is invited to see James W. Silver's *Mississippi: The Closed Society* (New York: Harcourt, Brace, and World, Inc., 1963–64) and Russell H. Barrett's *Integration at Ole Miss* (Chicago: Quadrangle Books, 1965).

12. Televised address urging support of a proposed constitutional amendment lowering voter registration requirements. The amendment passed by a three-to-one majority referendum—a defeat for the KKK and White Citizens Council—a vote of confidence for the Governor. While the clear motive was to offset the illiterate Negro bloc vote by an illiterate bloc vote of 400,000 unregistered Caucasians, the ground rules were in a lawful, honest setting.

13. Governor Coleman was sworn in as Judge of the 5th Circuit Court of Appeals (New Orleans) on August 16, 1965, strongly supported by Senator James Eastland and Attorney General Katzenbach, as a segregationist who had stood for law and order despite his segregationist views. But the bitter cup of decision had passed from him.

14. Cleary, *op. cit.*, p. 30, quoted from "Statewide Address on Television and Radio," September 13, 1962 (mimeographed) as reprinted in *Race Relations Law Reporter* 7 (1962), p. 748. (Nashville, Tennessee: Vanderbilt University, Law School.)

15. Cleary, *op. cit.*, p. 31.

16. Whatever history may record, this moment is believed by many to have put Johnson into the Governor's chair in the next election. The chivalrous slogan of "Stand tall with Paul" was used in his successful campaign against former Governor James P. Coleman. Long afterward, the contempt charges against Barnett and Johnson were dropped, because punishment would no longer serve "any useful purpose." The calculated stance of those years may be attributed to the then strong, now weak, political forces of the White Citizens Council.

17. *The Race Relations Law Reporter*, published at Vanderbilt University, Nashville, Tennessee, illustrates the copious continuing nature of litigation.

18. The contributions of Jerre S. Williams, the Rex G. Baker Professor of Law at the University of Texas Law School, have been of immense help on this topic. His addresses to the Southern Association of Colleges and Schools, in 1963 and 1964, published in the *Proceedings* of those years, provide a definitive account of desegregation and the law in higher education.

19. Jerre S. Williams, "The Implications of the Civil Rights Act of 1964." Address before the college delegate assembly at the Southern Association of Colleges and Schools, December 2, 1964, in Memphis, Tennessee, and published in the 1964 *Proceedings* of the Association.

20. *Ibid.*

4. Forces for Change

In considering the qualitative aspects of desegregation, and its institutional dimensions, we encounter two distinct problems. These will be evident in giving our present attention to regional leadership agencies and to the forces of change at the institutional level. First of all, in the more sensitive research areas, there is what we might label the "Phenomenon of Inverse Significance," referring to the inverse relationship between the significance of a fact and the freedom to document it in a conventional scholarly manner. Privileged information is often the most revealing of the crucial elements of an issue or problem, but carries its "off-the-record" footnoting taboo, as many social science researchers can freely attest.

Secondly, there is the subjective matter of ascribing motives to observable behavior. It is both hazardous and unfair to impugn motives because, with differing goals and with varying perceptions of ways to achieve them, events are often not what they appear to be. Prudence may be mistaken for weakness; courage for cowardice. "Wrong" things are done for the "right" reasons; "right" things for unworthy purposes. Yet, the obligation for candor and integrity remains in describing significant relevant events. This dual responsibility poses a problem both for the author and for the reader, who like to call (what is perceived to be) a "spade a spade." Some motives appear to be transparent, while others seem inscrutable, but we can never be quite sure which are which. Together, we will have to do the best we can.

I. FORCES AT THE REGIONAL LEVEL

The South has long been organized to do business on a regional basis.[1] That has often been its genius of strength and, at times, its weakness.[2] In the desegregation era of higher education, the fact is

41

abundantly clear that major first steps could not have been taken without a collective commitment within southern organizations combined with the support and sanction of individuals, and of private and governmental agencies outside the South.

Reference was made in the opening chapter of this report to the roles of regional organizations in the early years of desegregation in higher education, the years in which major cracks appeared in southern higher education customs. During the ensuing years, since 1954, each of those organizations has had a major part in subsequent developments, sometimes as a force of change, sometimes as a respondent to it; sometimes promoting desegregation, sometimes seeming almost oblivious to it while studying and working at other significant issues and tasks of higher education. Together, these forces have managed to converge with over-all good effect.

The Southern Regional Council

From its origin, in 1944, the Council has regarded segregation as an unconscionable barrier to economic progress, to personal dignity, and to social welfare generally. Its major tactic, however, has been the discovery of facts which illustrate the enormity of injustice attending segregation and confronting—sometimes arousing—the citizenry with facts which have changed their thought and action patterns. Yet it is not accurate to say that desegregation *per se* has ever been the end goal of the Council. It has been viewed, instead, as an essential step toward dealing with other problems of injustice, in the varied forms of inequality of opportunity.

In 1966, though continuing to perform something of the same basic informative and action stirring function, it is no longer regarded as the strong "left wing" organization, a common earlier epithet to which it became accustomed. Indeed, the Council now has real cause for concern about some "ultra-liberal" groups which appear to be callous to the shattering side effects of civil disobedience, designed only to achieve the limited goal of desegregation. Many of the civil rights demonstrations have been authentic examples of Mahatma Gandhi's conception of civil disobedience. Others have been grotesque distortions of the principle of civil disobedience. The Council's course has been to work untiringly for desegregation, sensitized to those side effects which may promote or impede equal opportunity in its deeper sense.

The Council's activities since 1954 have focused more upon the matter of public school desegregation than on desegregation at the higher educational level. Information obtained and disseminated by the Council to various "keep the schools open" groups throughout the South has made a deep imprint on decision-making. (Many southerners will recall the S. O. S. ["Save Our Schools"] movement, and comparable groups which leaned on the Council for a variety of data and contacts.)

Its work continues in other areas. For example, its recent report on "Southern Justice: An Indictment," is a carefully documented study on the continuing double standard of justice.[3] While the Council's focus of attention through these years has not been principally upon higher education, its behind the scenes influence has been considerable. There has been no public doubt of its commitment to desegregation in higher education. It has been available to "turn to." Its sustained effort in this direction has resulted in a major impact beyond what documented footnotes could convey. As an official of the Council once expressed it, "It has been our job to be a public target for the segregationists while protecting the anonymity of our friends and supporters who have a great deal at stake with their families and businesses in this movement." To some degree, officials of the Council in earlier years had to lose "caste" by their outspoken position. In 1966 they are regarded as being among the more or less respected moderates.[4]

The Southern Education Reporting Service

Soon after the decision of the U. S. Supreme Court on May 17, 1954, declaring compulsory segregation in the public schools unconstitutional, an urgent need was felt by many journalists, educators, and other citizens to establish a news medium which would publish the comprehensive, relevant facts about desegregation without fear or favor. The Southern Education Reporting Service proved to be a worthy response to that social need.

SERS, as it has familiarly come to be called, was established by journalists and educators with the South "with the aim of providing accurate, unbiased information to school administrators, public officials, and interested lay citizens on developments in education arising from that Supreme Court decision."[5]

Southern School News, in September 1954, became the official monthly publication of the Southern Education Reporting Service and performed the exceedingly significant function for a decade of separating fact from fancy, of replacing ignorance with knowledge in an emotionally charged area where there was such a "need to know." The *News* reported upon developments in public higher education as well as in the public schools, thereby enabling interested educators and citizens, whatever their beliefs, to read the rapidly unfolding manifestations of changing social realities rather than being able only to conjecture about them. The first officers of the Service were Virginius Dabney, Thomas R. Waring, and

C. A. McKnight who, with an able Board of Directors and correspondents, set the agency on a true course.

The publication of the *Southern School News* was discontinued with the June 1965 issue, being succeeded by a bimonthly publication, the *Southern Education Report*, established to report on programs for educating culturally disadvantaged children and youth in southern and border states. The SERS, however, will continue to maintain much of its data-gathering services concerning desegregation in public education on all levels.

Over the eleven years of its reporting service, covering seventeen Southern and border states, and the District of Columbia, the Southern Education Reporting Service has had an incalculable impact upon the strategy and tactics governing desegregation in higher education. Information has minimized the malignant effects of propaganda. In 1966, under the combined leadership of its Chairman, Chancellor Alexander Heard of Vanderbilt University, Managing Editor John Popham of the *Chattanooga Times*, and its Executive Director, Robert Campbell, and with a capable and deeply committed Board of Directors, the Southern Education Reporting Service continues its strategic yeomanly service in the South's alliance for truth. The desegregation era has been helped along in a way that attests to the faith that knowing the truth is apt to make us free.

The Southern Education Foundation

The perspective of this Foundation has been one which has placed its faith and its resources in the value of research concerning social problems and in the value of relevant further education, mainly to promising Negro leadership within the South. The Southern Education Foundation has taken a "long view" of progress. It has not openly sought to pry open the doors of desegregation, but has availed itself of opportunities to develop a climate of support of it, and to help the practice of desegregation succeed within whatever prevailing restrictions were connected with it.

Its tactic has been characteristically that of gentle suasion. In 1954–55, for example, George Peabody College for Teachers admitted some of its first Negro graduate students who attended the college with the aid of SEF grants. The following year the University of Oklahoma did likewise. A decade later, the budget of the Southern Education Foundation included grants for Negro graduate students, with only four exceptions, in each of the state universities of the South. The Foundation's shift of support during the height of the desegregation era turned toward a "Leadership Development Program" including regional summer programs and full year fellowships at more than a score of southern institutions. Aware of the growing need to assist Negro education in both the historically Caucasian and the historically Negro institutions, its support has gone to such institutions as Atlanta University and Tuskegee Institute as well as to such others as the University of Arkansas and the University of Texas.[6]

The size of the grants for such a herculean regional task was small indeed: 1954–55, $170,000; 1959–60, $210,000; 1964–65, $350,000.[7] The personal work of the small staff of the Foundation, however, generated a great deal of hope and stirred career ambitions among capable Negroes and multiplied the effect of the limited funds that were directly expended. Many beneficiaries of the program, working in increasingly responsible positions of leadership in segregated and desegregated environments, attest to the assurance that the Foundation showed that it cared about them as people as well as about the wider societal objectives which the Foundation and its beneficiaries shared.

Some current analyses of racial problems point to the South as a region of hope for accelerated progress because of the calibre of responsible leadership among educated Negroes. These analyses express concern about the remainder of America because of its relative lack of such leadership. Our purpose here is not to examine the validity of that position.[8] The fact is clear, however, that the strategy of the Southern Education Foundation in avoiding a direct confrontation with the wall of segregation by going around it or nudging it a little here and there, has made secure a relevant education for Negro leadership, alert and sensitive to changing social realities. To have been another Southern Regional Council would not have squared with, but would have distracted it from its vision of educational service through and beyond desegregation. Yet without the *avant garde* efforts of the Council, the work of the Foundation might have been of little avail. Each played specialized and significant roles.

The Southern Regional Education Board

The work of the SREB during the desegregation era has been quite broad in its scope of research and service. Its course has been steered by a variety of considerations, and it has not regarded the direct furtherance of desegregation to be within its purview. As the Southern Regional Council placed an accent on desegregation, and the Southern Education Foundation focused on extended opportunity for Negroes in segregated and desegregated contexts, the SREB has assumed a massive responsibility for improving a balance, and a qualitative soundness of higher education generally throughout the South. While its support and special historical reason for existence derives from the interest of public higher education, it has worked actively with private institutions of higher learning as well.

On the one hand, it has strengthened and given substance to centers of excellence in specialized areas of graduate and professional schools, enabling the South to overcome some areas of major deficiencies and to reduce the waste of resources and duplicated effort from state to state. Notable among its achievements are those in the areas of medicine, dentistry, veterinary medicine, social work, public health, and special education. In the academic year 1964–65, for example, the SREB disbursed $1,815,000 for contracts with twenty-one regional institutions for admitting 1,200 students from fifteen states in these areas.[9]

Student aid contracts, in addition, have been transmitted without regard to race through the SREB for students in the field of forestry, architecture, library science, and actuarial science. The effort has been directed to the hope that no competent student will be denied the opportunity to achieve his educational goals by the barrier of segregation or by virtue of his ethnic origin. The emotionally charged issues of desegregation, as John Ivey had posited years earlier, were not to detract the Board from its central purpose of strengthening educational programs and extending educational opportunities in higher education, within existing political restrictions as the Board reviewed them.

In 1961, the SREB created a Commission on Goals for Higher Education in the South to take a broad look at the multi-faceted nature of goal fulfillment of southern institutions of higher education. The Commission consisted of such southern leaders as Colgate Darden (Chairman), Ralph McGill, and the late A. Boyd Campbell, one-time President of the U. S. Chamber of Commerce. The Commission arrived at five broad goals of higher education, including that of guiding the region in solving "social problems created by population changes, racial differences, urbanization, and technological growth."[10]

Directly and publicly, therefore, the Southern Regional Education Board has not viewed the issues of desegregation as being among its chief concerns. Nonetheless, it has accomplished many educational tasks which could not conceivably have been accomplished by the simple expedient of desegregation alone. Its *modus operandi*, since its origin, has been to avoid entanglement with these issues and to get on with other major problems of southern higher education. Some have argued, with merit, that the Board should have faced desegregation issues openly and squarely. Yet none can cogently impugn the motives of the Board nor detract from the outstanding contributions, in other areas, that it has made.

The Southern Association of Colleges and Schools

The years of 1954–55 were years of ambiguity for the Southern Association relative to its own desegregation. The times called for a man of stature, of conviction, and of vision to emerge. One did. In 1955, at the Association's Convention in Miami Beach, Florida, the sole survivor among the founders of the Southern Association, then nearly eighty years of age, rose to the occasion of that new day. Professor Emeritus Edwin Mims, of Vanderbilt University, challenged that assembly of educators with these words: "We seem to be letting matters drift to some kind of catastrophe ... Do you realize that we are in some states on the verge of nullification and even secession and of advocating a policy that would bring to naught all our efforts to build up a well-integrated school system? Who are the leaders in this organization to take up the unfinished work of Haygood, Dillard, Jackson Davis and many others who have worked at this problem?"[11]

According to W. H. McEniry, one of many men who did take up this unfinished work, Dr. Mims' vision, and the respect his life had commanded "brought nearly two thousand men and women to their feet in spontaneous applause when he had finished speaking."[12]

Applause was significant as a revelation of sentiment of a person, and for the views he championed. It was no substitute, however, for the controversial, tedious, and plain hard work that lay ahead. The following year, in 1956, the Southern Association approved full membership for Negro colleges and universities which met the standards of the Commission on Colleges of the Southern Association. During the next five years, various philanthropies and other organizations showed themselves to be allies in a cause of achieving a kind of institutional equality of opportunity. The United Negro College Fund, the Southern Fellowship Fund, the General Education Board, the Southern Education Foundation, and the Danforth Foundation were principal among them.

The support of the Danforth Foundation provides an appropriate example of this assistance. The Southern Association provided for a gradual transition toward a desegregated organization over a five-year period. Thus any historically Negro college might be visited, for purposes of accreditation and Association membership, from 1957 to 1962, when the "approved lists (Class A)" of Negro colleges would be discontinued. The Danforth Foundation selected twenty-eight such institutions and proceeded to assist them financially to improve their facilities, staff, and program to measure up to the higher standards of the Association. As the Foundation reports with justifiable pride, "When the target date arrived, January 1, 1962, twenty-six of the twenty-eight colleges that the Foundation had assisted in this program made the grade of full accreditation."[13]   It was one thing to open the door at the top of the stairs. It was quite another to help disadvantaged institutions to climb them.

A total of forty-five Negro colleges were fully accredited by, and thereby members of, the Southern Association at the end of 1961.[14]   The Association, meanwhile, had been concerned about the quantitative emphasis of its accreditation standards rather than the concept of qualitative growth.   Its leaders were concerned about the issue of desegregation, but their thoughts placed desegregation in a perspective of relevance and quality in higher education.   Largely in deference to the integration of the Association, it postponed a modification of accreditation standards until the institutional phase of desegregation was complete.   In November, 1962, the College Delegate Assembly adopted the new Standards of Accreditation designed to measure more adequately the quality of educational programs with less reliance on quantitative criteria.[15]

The Association has now become fully desegregated in policy and in fact.   It has become so in a growing context of cooperation, and has on occasion—as in the University of Mississippi racial crisis—assumed a posture of courage as an agent of change, in brooking no further political interference in educational affairs.   By 1965 it had moved forward in exercising its chief function of accreditation, and its service functions of consultation, stimulation, and initiation of worthy educational projects.   As it had done from the beginning of the desegregation era, however, the Association has attempted to study the inherent ramifications of the issues of desegregation in the over-all interest of individuals, educational institutions, and societal needs.   In this strategy of gradualism, within its own framework of the democratic process, its evolutionary development has proceeded without rupturing relationships, as revolutions tend to do.   The Association is in a favorable position in 1966 to look ahead to the postdesegregation era in a constructive manner and with a substantially unified spirit.

The Net Effect of Regional Organizations

The purposes and foci of action of the organizations cited above have been quite different and largely independent of each other. All of them have been committed to worthy purposes, and their collective efforts have converged toward the aims of higher education which embrace the goals of desegregation, but go beyond the view that physical desegregation, in a legalistic sense, is a true end goal. These agencies for equalizing and extending opportunity have recognized, all along, that mere desegregation within the law is only a kind of fools' gold, and leads only to an illusory hope. Each in its own way has moved higher education along, through the desegregation era, to a social system that remains intact and is now in a position to look and move toward the broader considerations of higher education in a changing America. As they have worked, they have endured together the criticisms of moving too fast, too slow, or not at all; of skirting issues or confronting them without sensitivity; of having the wrong purposes or employing faulty means in achieving them. Yet they have endured, and continue at their tasks.

II. FORCES OF CHANGE WITHIN THE COLLEGES

Regional organizations and agencies have been central in stabilizing, generating, and giving direction to change in southern higher education. Yet they have not been the only external influences, by any means, which have significantly modified collegiate life.

Many other forces have also impinged upon desegregation in southern higher education. Church conventions have gone both ways, for and against the movement. The press has wrestled with its ethical conscience, some newsmen and editors seeking to be loyal to the public-service responsibility of keeping the citizens factually informed, some more loyal to the commercial motives of "good copy" for circulation and, in turn, advertising expansion. The work of Chambers of Commerce and other economically oriented groups has been significant. Some supportive efforts of private foundations have been previously cited. Sometimes their policy of making grants only to integrated institutions has been conducive to desegregation and to good side effects attending it. At other times, such policies have been interpreted as bribery and have blocked a potential for developing empathy in some delicate areas of opportunity. The work of "SNICK" (the Student Non-Violent Coordinating Committee) has had a militant effect on college students and upon higher education generally, with a net evaluation defying demonstrable effects.

With these and other external forces in operation, the key questions remain: "What is happening within each institution where some degree of desegregation is an accomplished fact? What are the shaping forces beyond the achievement of mere physical proximity of Negro and non-Negro students in institutions of higher learning? In short, what forces of change are evident on the college campus, promoting desegregation or retarding it?

In our visits to a wide variety of Southern colleges and universities, the staff of this study have heard many things and seen some others.

We lay no claim to having a "sanitary statistical sample" of conditions, but we have come close to seeing the full range of them in many respects. The present description of shaping forces at the collegiate level is admittedly and deliberately distorted in favor of positive examples of prudence rather than of the negative forces that are still at work against the interests of educational opportunity and human dignity. We must show the negative side as well, but we shall not dwell upon it.

The vignettes of action shown in the subsequent pages of this chapter were obtained, in part, as privileged information. To avoid identification where it may be embarrassing, some disguise of details of data, but not of substantive fact, will be intentional. In other instances, identity will be thinly enough veiled that some readers may recognize the referenced institution. All institutions will be referred to as colleges, but some are not.

College Administrators

To a large degree the chief executive official of the institution sets the tone of its internal climate. Sometimes he may be a compliant servant of his Board. Sometimes he virtually controls it. Hopefully, most of the time he is in a partnership relationship with it. Some new presidents have made explicit the conditions on which they were willing to serve.[16] Others, to become president, have chosen not to view their role as influencing policy but only as administering it. While there are distressing exceptions, presidents are generally working at the impossible task of administering a going business, improving an educational enterprise, pleasing or placating various publics, and accomplishing desegregation, more or less.

Situation A (1964)

In a report to his faculty, staff, and students, the president of Berry College, in Mt. Berry, Georgia, outlined the moral issues involving segregation and supported a nondiscriminatory policy. He, and others, had taken steps toward such a policy since 1959. While the institution's official admission policy made no reference to race, institutional practice had long implied the rejection of applications for Negroes, and no applications had been previously submitted.

His second supportive position was a financial one. He pointed out that such a nonpublic, and nonaffluent institution ran the risk of eliminating itself from consideration for grants from the major foundations and from federal funds. Some current funds, already half encumbered, would no longer be available.

For these reasons in combination, the president announced, at the close of the first day of classes in September, 1964, that he had personally sought and recruited three Negro students who had been admitted to the college, and would attend classes beginning the next day. These quotations from his remarks state his position, his empathy, and his tactics:

> I realize that some of you [students], or perhaps some of your parents, may be in fundamental disagreement with the action I have deemed best in your interest and that of our institution. I hope that persons in disagreement with this action find it possible to adjust sufficiently their personal feelings to the facts of a rapidly changing world. If any of those students prefer not to attend [this institution] under these new circumstances, their full charges for tuition, fees, and room will be refunded . . . [but, he added, there are few other segregated places to go].
>
> It is better to face change and to get on with the job at hand than to be caught in the web of floundering resistance. Let us proceed honestly and with dignity. We must treat all students with hospitality for which our college is justly proud. Let us . . . show that we can assure responsible action in these grave matters of human relations.[17]

Situation B (1964)

This institution, in Louisiana, provided an example of unprovable resistance to the admission of fourteen Negro students. The institution was fully eligible for federal funds, and had received some foundation grants as an "integrated" institution. The administration had an unwritten policy, understood by faculty and students alike, that Negro students were to be tolerated, but otherwise ignored. The practice was, in the corridors for example, "to look through Negroes as if they just weren't there." The white students who felt differently, however few or many, felt this administrative taboo against personal greetings and discussions even on academic matters between Negro students and themselves. There were no physical rails marked "for colored only" around the Negroes as there had been at the University of Oklahoma for Professor McLaurin years earlier, but the social rails and markings were quite as real. Nowhere could be better illustrated the spurious goal of desegregation as its own end.

Situation C (1964)

The administration team of another college, a state university branch, was publicly and privately committed to the concept of desegregation and equal opportunity. This was in a state that forbade "social" desegregation, at the edge of the city cited by John Steinback in his *Travels with Charlie* as being the low point of his "search of

America" because of the unmotherly invectives screamed against de-segregated colored pupils there—the middle-aged "cheerleaders." This college, despite that outer environment, was, on campus, an epitome of individual dignity in academic and social relationships.   To see and hear a desegregated seminar of student teachers engaged together in the analysis of public education, unrelated to race, showed convincingly what the subculture within a college campus can achieve, given the posi-tive sanction of its visible power structure.   To see those young adults walk out of that class, in desegregated and segregated pairs, and some cheerfully alone, showed that ethnic comradery can flower anywhere it can find a small plot of cultivated, fertile soil and a favorable social climate.

Situation D (1960)

The president of this church-connected college in Texas was com-mitted to a strategy of gradualism in general, and to gradualism in the desegregation of facilities and services in particular.[18]   The barber-shop was the "last to go," and the president, while getting his own hair cut, made a personal plea to the college barber to serve Negro students. The barber demurred, saying that he didn't know how to cut a Negro's hair. He reluctantly agreed, however, to try.

A Negro student soon came in. He was treated courteously, and the barber spent longer than usual in an effort to do a creditable job. The student was disappointed with the results, but he was convinced of the barber's willingness to try. After that, the student returned to a Negro barber who could do a more satisfactory job. The president, in this and other ways, worked as a kind of personal shock absorber in the anticipation of problems. Caucasian and Negro students who are en-rolled there now report a genuine sense of equality and, with apologies for the overused term, a sense of "community."

The College Faculty

Individually and collectively, the college faculty have been the catalysts in many internal dimensions of change. They have provided the students, in a context of desegregation, with cues of encouragement. They have, however, sometimes found difficulty in defining for them-selves a role which has made them both intellectually and emotionally assured that they were right. For example, is compensatory grading ethical? "Of course not," the mind replies. "Hold on a minute," pleads the heart.

Situation E (1963)

At this private, historically Negro institution in Alabama, the faculty wished to give moral encouragement to students to "demonstrate" in the Civil Rights movement if they regarded this as a proper civic responsibility or opportunity. With faculty support, institutional policy permitted students to cut classes for such purposes without penalty. The college could not "go their bail," of course, for financial and other reasons, but the faculty would assure that students were not academically handicappted by exercising what they considered to be their civic obligation. This was kind of "a laboratory for citizenship," and SNCC recruited a goodly share of demonstrators from the institution.

The experiment was not without disillusionment. Marginal or failing students began cutting classes, along with other students, in the hope that their participation in demonstrations would pull their grades up to a passing level. The faculty learned quickly, and students already on academic probation or in marginal standing were denied eligibility for this "free cut" privilege. If good academic standing could be required for participation in interscholastic athletics, the point was argued, it might also apply reasonably to intercollegiate demonstrations. Students could no longer "make a good thing" out of them.

College F (1955)

This historically Negro college, located in a border state west of Virginia, received a number of applications for admission from non-resident students who sought to transfer from a nearby Caucasian college. College F had earned and enjoyed a good reputation for its excellent faculty and its high academic standards. Reports were received, by "grapevine," that the Caucasian students were largely motivated by a desire to get some "crip courses," and transfer their credits back to their original alma mater. If the Negro faculty applied a double standard in favor of non-Negroes, they might be able to attract more Caucasian students and unify their standards later. If not, they might lose forever their awaited chance to become a genuinely desegregated institution. They chose the difficult, latter course.

On this single standard of grading, numerous Caucasian students received poor grades; a few earned and received good ones. Most became early dropouts. Over the years, however, the word spread that the quality of instruction was good, and that standards were "uniformly" high. The institution now numbers its non-Negro students in the hundreds. The faculty itself, long since desegregated, has been able to learn, and to teach, some fundamental lessons of equality of educational opportunity—helping students to succeed, but never pretending that failure is success. That faculty discovered that integrity pays practical dividends.

Situation G

The public college president in this state was averse to desegregation and used a variety of administrative stalls to delay or contain it. The liberal faculty, however, formed a relentless pressure for admission and educational opportunity without reference to race. Reinforced by a growing community sentiment for it, the president, then near retirement, at last yielded. It was in substantial fact a faculty victory for access to higher education opportunity. Two years later, the administrator, upon the public occasion of his retirement, received the conventional accolades and made a few farewell remarks. Among others, he announced that the achievement of his administration about which he felt the deepest pride was the effective, orderly, and complete desegregation of his college. As he anticipated, he received a tremendous round of applause. Many never knew.

The Student Body

The collegiate spotlight has been thrown upon the college student since the widely publicized Berkeley case, and subsequent dramatic actions of student groups from California to Boston. These demonstrations are commonly among those students outside the duly elected representatives, the student council, etc. Our situations here, in contrast, show the positive, constructive action of duly constituted student groups rather than the self-appointed "rump groups" which, while getting on the agenda of the American Council of Education, are not representative of the majority of students for whom they presume to speak. The South, of course, has been atypical from the standpoint of "normative" collegiate demonstrative behavior. Student protests and constructive action have tended to find expression through existing channels rather than around them. Student leaders from southern colleges explain it this way: "We are not in search of causes. Maybe we ought to be. Our problem is student apathy about causes when we bump into them. The Administration will usually give us a hearing, and will work something out, or we will be told why. We are apt to respect duly constituted authority even when we think administrators are in error or 'fuddy-duddy.' We can understand some of their old-fashioned views, and besides, we can find ways around the walls of security they put up if it's that important. We don't have to break

them down." To date the record in the South shows that students un-
aided by faculty sympathies, as at the University of Tennessee, do not
find that demonstrations succeed. In Knoxville, the intemperate anti-
administration protests were quickly subdued, with a community
"assist" from the daily press.

College H (1962)

While previous efforts to desegregate public collegiate institutions
in this particular state had been unsuccessful, the prospect seemed to be
a foregone conclusion that it would be accomplished there. The college
student council was divided on the issue of desegregation. They were
not divided, however, on the need to keep their institutional social
system intact by living up to their obligation to duly established regulations.

When informed by the Dean of Students that the college would
soon admit its first Negro student, and that there would be more,
students assumed responsibility for making clear their stance of support
to all students. Students were advised that, if they could not abide
by that decision without stirring up trouble, they should not plan to
re-enroll after Christmas. The decisive nature of the college's policy
was not left in doubt.

The student body, despite some strong segregationist sentiment,
stood fast on the position of respect for regulations, even resisting and
"informing" on subsequent efforts of White Citizens Council visitors,
"incognito," who attempted to infiltrate in order to create an incident.
The student body, knowing it could count on firm support from the
faculty and administration, achieved a man-made miracle by its resolute
action.

One student who made his desegregation successful was the first
Negro student himself. Academically able, and personally sensitive
to the delicacy of the problem, he did his part, too. He neither lived
the role of a "privileged character" nor that of a subservient nephew
of "Uncle Tom." He was able to relax and even joke about the problem
of which he was a part without repudiating either himself as a person
or his race for which he held high esteem.

Situation I (1965)

Within one southern metropolis, a Collegiate Exchange Council
of students was formed, representing predominantly Negro and predominantly Caucasian institutions. It did not enjoy the unqualified
support of all of the presidents of the represented institutions. Yet it
moved ahead. The Constitution outlined these aims of the Council:

1. To exchange ideas on student government and student government projects and problems.
2. To encourage closer ties of understanding among the institutions.
3. To coordinate and cosponsor collegiate programs and activities.

One of the first projects of this group was the printing of a joint collegiate publication for dissemination among all affiliated colleges. With assistance and imaginative guidance, such an intercollegiate body can become, in that city and others, a significant shaping force in higher education far beyond the conditions of merely advancing desegregation.

Situation J (1964)

Three students and two faculty members, at the University of Virginia, conducted a poll of student attitudes about Negroes, under the auspices of the county chapter of the Virginia Council on Human Relations. The purpose of the poll was a bit devious, perhaps even Machiavellian. If results proved unfavorable to the Negro, they would not be publicized, but the chapter would institute an education program to effect attitudinal change. If favorable, the results would be published to assure the Negro that he was regarded as welcomed in the university community.

Questionnaires were mailed to a random fourth of the student body (1,450), and 1,045 responses (72%) were received. Among the respondents, 85% fully approved of permitting Negro students to enrol in the university, and more than 72% believed that Negro students should be treated as "any other student." Yet, more than 3% were openly antagonistic; a few obscene. Similar polls had been taken on two occasions in previous years, and this poll revealed a continuing increase of acceptance of desegregation. Sixty percent approved the idea of a desegregated faculty.[19]

III. CONCLUDING OBSERVATIONS

The shaping forces of desegregation and beyond have varied greatly in nature, in magnitude, and in strategy. We have considered some of these forces, but have by no means exhausted their number nor explored these forces in real depth. The desegregation era, due to the combined operation of the many forces that have given it shape and substance, has come virtually to an end, in its legislative compliance sense. There will continue to be a few instances of *de facto* segregated institutions in public and nonpublic higher education. It is important to remember that some will remain so, more as a matter of principle, as they view it, than due either to stubbornness or opportunism.[20] The "expedient" institutions have largely joined the ranks of desegregated institutions, along with those which have done so out of moral compunction.

Shaping forces, as we have considered them, may take the form of external, organizational action; or they may find expression in the single act of an individual—a president, a professor, or a student—acting alone or in concert. All of us are potential agents of change, and each of us is a member of a number of power groups, ert or inert; we are forces of change, for inertia or against it, for better or for worse.

REFERENCES

1. To stretch this point, the Southern Bell Telephone & Telegraph Company carries, in its Atlanta directory more than 400 listings of firms and organizations beginning with the words "Southern" or "Southeastern" from churches to liquor companies.

2. Consider, for example, the Southern Governors' Conference and its Regional Education Board on the one hand, and the Ku Klux Klan on the other; or the Southern Association of Colleges and Schools on the one hand and the White Citizens' Private School Association on the other.

3. Published by the Southern Regional Council and the American Civil Liberties Union, October 8, 1965. Publications are available from the Council at 5 Forsyth Street, Atlanta, Georgia. There is little doubt that this and comparable studies influenced the President to declare, in his State of the Union address on January 12, 1966, that civil rights legislation must be directed toward eradicating discrimination in the selection of jurors, and in other *prima facie* evidences of double standards of justice.

4. Interviews, off the record and undated. Personal contacts have been maintained since 1959.

5. *Southern School News*, October 1, 1954 (Nashville: Southern Education Reporting Service, Box 6156, Acklen Station). From the beginning the Service has been financially supported by grants from the Ford Foundation, now exceeding $2,000,000, and aided by modest income from subscriptions.

6. Southern Education Foundation, Inc., Preliminary Statements of the Executive Director (unpublished) in Annual Budget Dockets, 1958–59 through 1964–65, inclusive.

7. *Ibid.*

8. A report on "The Fast Changing South" (*Look*, 29:23 [November 16, 1965]) purported to explain why the South may solve its problems "sooner than the North or West." The point, however, is how the South and North and West may learn from each other (instead of instructing each other) so that America may solve its fundamental

ethnic problems more readily and more genuinely.

9. *SREB, 1964–65*, 130 Sixth Street, N.W., Atlanta, Georgia. Contracts for Services allow a state which does not offer a specialized program to send its students to other states to receive it. The selected institutions receive, thereby, qualified students and added financial support.

10. *Within our Reach* (Atlanta: Southern Regional Education Board, 1961), p. 9.

11. W. H. McEniry, "Educational Progress in the Southern States," an address delivered before the Association of Colleges and Schools, December, 1961, p. 4.

12. *Ibid.*

13. *The Danforth Foundation Annual Report, 1963–64* (St. Louis: The Danforth Foundation, 1964), p. 7.

14. McEniry, *op. cit.*, p. 6. (The number climbed to fifty-three in 1964.)

15. "General Accrediation in Higher Education: A Statement from the Staff of the Commission on Colleges" (Atlanta: Southern Association of Colleges and Schools, 1963), p. 6.

16. One college president, and at least one chancellor, made clear their resolute determination not to flout or circumvent any law of the land. This was not easy. This kind of unheralded valor goes unnoted in the press, but shapes the strategy of southern higher education, nevertheless.

17. Mimeographed copy of the remarks of President J. R. Bertrand, and reproduced with his permission. Three white students withdrew; two, reportedly, were very homesick freshmen. Since June, 1965, three Negro coeds have enrolled as residential students. Others are attending as day students.

18. This observer notes that gradualism tends to be a personal trait which may embrace an attitude about desegregation. One may be duly skeptical, however, about an administrator who espouses gradualism in this area alone.

19. Gene Blumenreich and Jerry Coffey, "VCHR Opinion Poll," *Plume and Sword*, IV:10 (April 9, 1964).

20. A president of a church-related college, commonly classified as of fundamentalist faith, confided that he and his church constituency wanted a "like-minded" group of students—of "one accord" about religion, of the basic tenets of morality, and of "one body" about race. However strong or weak his position, he, his church, and their college have a legal right to uphold it. It is not hypocritical. It is sincere, unless he signs the Title VI Assurance of Compliance, which he has not. Others, with similar views, have done so.

5.

The Negro's Desegregation Dilemma

At the beginning of the desegregation era in southern higher education some educators held the utopian idealism that if desegregation could be achieved a great new brotherhood of man would evolve from it. This unsubstantiated faith found its opposite in the cynical outlook that desegregation itself would ruin the chances for congenial relations between the races because of the conflict that would inevitably be generated in the process. Through the years of desegregation, we have witnessed the disillusionment of many who placed their central hopes on desegregation itself. We have also seen that the dire predictions of the "super realists" did not materialize.

I. CONDITIONS ATTENDING DESEGREGATION

In order to understand desegregation in perspective, it is important to recognize three present conditions which have a direct bearing on the postdesegregation era. They may be overly magnified here, but there is a discomfiting authenticity about each of them.

The Condition of Diffused Action

Higher education, with reference to its avowed aims and potential, is among the most inert power groups for social action within the South. Yet, by virtue of the leadership of its two major regional organizations, the Southern Association of Colleges and Schools and the Southern Regional Education Board, it is better tooled for action than any other region in America. This lack of coordinated leadership for social action in the South is no one's fault in particular. The colleges are doing many good things.[1] The irony is that with trivial goodness and lack of coordinated effort, higher education has missed much of its opportunity to serve the interests of societal advancement, in both the material and nonmaterial spheres of its potential influence.

The impetus for the desegregation era serves as a cogent case in point. The colleges were in the vanguard of this era more by the initiative of the National Association for the Advancement of Colored People and the mandates of the highest tribunal in our judicial system than by initiative within the higher education establishment. Higher education cannot be generally charged, of course, with responsibility for effecting social change through overt action. In some cases, however, that is surely its function, one it has on occasion exercised. It does have the bounden duty, however, to take the initiative in developing a climate of concern and commitment in which socially responsible change is apt to be a natural consequence.

Broadus Butler, the Special Assistant of the U. S. Associate Commissioner for Higher Education, made the point forcibly that: "It is to the professors, the research scholars, and to the institutions of higher education that the nation must inevitably turn to seek the most studied and serious judgments about both domestic and international affairs. Even more important, it is in institutions of higher education that attitude formation of the most respected and authoritative order for good or bad reaches the highest degree of sophistication."[2] Southern higher education is not well coordinated for initiating societal change, but in the main, only slowly responds to it.

The Condition of Transitory Commitments

Higher education is chronically harassed by a growing pattern of transitory educational commitments. The financial lure of the moment governs the institution's way of life in large part because it has not functionally clarified its special reasons for existence. The tragedy is compounded, in ironic fashion, by governmental and private philanthropic agencies which are genuinely committed to the worthy causes to which institutions give sporadic attention. The federal government, up to 1966, has been uncertain, from year to year, of the nature and amount of resources it will invest in higher learning. The "guns and butter" State of the Union address in January, 1966, pledged a continuing commitment to education, despite the continuing Viet Nam crisis. The subsequent State of the Union rejoinder by the Grand Old Party urged increased domestic economies because of the Viet Nam drain on expenditures. Sustained commitments of higher education institutions cannot be predicated upon assumptions about political fortunes and the vagaries of public support. The federal government is almost forced into an untenable position of massive action based on hasty planning, of spending while the mood is right. The individual college cannot "bet on" sustained support in any of the major areas of educational programs.

Private foundations, on the contrary, have viewed their role as being initiators, or seed planters, but they have not stayed in the field, to use the farmer's words, to "lay the crops by"—to assure the harvest. Thus the institution needing to lean upon outside support is caught in the fashionable loyalty of the moment.

Desegregation again illustrates the condition. The era of desegregation, in the limited conventional sense of achieving the non-zero segregated circumstance, or a measure of tokenism beyond it, has been largely accomplished by the compelling force of law, the "withholding" policies of major foundations and the more recent provisions of Title VI of the Civil Rights Act of 1964. With a number of notable and laudable exceptions, these have been the true explanations of changes and the levels of commitment to them. They have been made, however, in harmony within a general context of transitory commitments, inexhorably reinforced by outside funding agencies.

The Condition of Desegregation Weariness

No matter which side of the struggle you are on, there are "just so many fights in a man." Southern institutions of higher education are weary from the travail of emotionally exhausting conflict. So, preoccupied with strategy and tactics, southern higher education is in a state of undeclared truce. Throughout this era, a kind of postponement of educational progress has been evident, and the desegregation business was only one of several causes. A few institutional planners are now looking ahead to the postdesegregation era, but the number is pathetically few. Among some of the predominantly Caucasian institutions, the Assurance of Compliance and a few highly visible athletes and/or scholars will "handle the situation" for the time being. Among others, the will to desegregate is genuine, but qualified Negro applicants are scarce and in artificially inflated demand. With contrasting purposes, the visible results are nearly the same. The predominantly Negro institutions are weary, too, as the subsequent chapter will explain. Among the predominantly Negro institutions, the more elite among them are growing as rapidly as they wish, and modest efforts to attract non-Negro students and faculty continue. In the main, however, desegregation as an observable fact has seemed to reach a quantitative plateau on which it may remain, for better or for worse. Some institutions, like Fisk University, aspire to increase their non-Negro enrollment manyfold —in Fisk's case from ten to a hundred.

II. ASSESSING THE EFFECTS OF DESEGREGATION

Two major limitations inherent in assessing the effects of desegregation must be publicly mentioned both in the interest of scholarship and in common fairness. First of all, the meaning any of us get from a fact or event is determined, in part, by the meaning or mind set that we take to that fact. These examples will suffice to cite the problem:

1. A Negro student is admitted to a fraternity at Stanford University, and is given widespread national publicity in connection with it. What are the effects of desegregation suggested by this fact?

2. Tougaloo College, predominantly Negro, in Jackson, Mississippi, has practiced faculty desegregation since 1869, and student desegregation since 1961. What are the effects of these facts? How do we assess them?

3. The Woodrow Wilson Internship Program, and cooperative arrangements between non-Southern institutions and Southern institutions have brought numerous young Caucasian professors into historically Negro colleges. Some are humble; some condescending; some haughty. The fact of cooperation makes good copy, good images. Is the net effect good?

4. A personnel recruiter for an electric power company in Michigan was recently in Tennessee to recruit Negro electrical engineers, visiting Fisk and Tennessee A & I universities, but not Vanderbilt or the University of Tennessee, because he did not come South to consider Caucasian candidates. He could get them from other institutions, most of them within the Midwest. He was getting racial and regional balance, recruiting only Negroes from the South. What are the effects of such a policy?

5. A church-connected institution became desegregated, but denied admission to the daughter of the local NAACP official presumably on the grounds that she did not qualify by the objective non-discriminatory standards. He concurred and commended the institution for its fairness.

However these and other events are assessed, a good deal more information is needed before a fair appraisal of effects can be concluded, and we are apt to read our own assessment into events conditioned by our personal prior value system.

The second major hazard in assessing effects of the desegregation era is the classic truism that "correlation does not prove causality." No matter how closely observable effects run along together, we can never be certain of particularistic causes. We can only study the patterns of change, and get the best judgments available in ascribing effects to causes. In the face of these two hazards of assessment, there is an impelling need to undertake a serious appraisal of desegregation's effects upon the Negro student, for whose benefit it was largely championed.

III. SELF-CONCEPTS AND ACADEMIC LEARNING

A spirited interview with a group of outstanding seniors at the Virginia State College unfolded revealing personal histories. Some of them, who volunteered for part-time teaching in the re-opening of the Prince Edward County schools, derived a deep sense of empathy and achievement from that experience. Some of the Negro students, having lived their lives in a segregated environment, explained how anxious and insecure they would yet feel in teaching in open competition with Caucasian teachers. As children they had been told, some of them, that Negroes were in fact inferior to Caucasians. Others had learned that it would be better for them to "act as if they felt inferior" to keep out of trouble and from being taken for an "uppity Nigra." Throughout their school and college lives, virtually all of them had been deprived of an opportunity to determine what they would be able to do in an open society. They were able by every measure available, but they were unsure of themselves in an open, desegregated society.

West Virginia State College represents a genuine model in desegregation, where both a desegregated student body and a desegregated faculty have developed a tradition over more than a decade that a man or woman is to be judged on his individual merits without reference to race. Not even there, of course, should we assume that racial consciousness and racial prejudice no longer exist. There have been occasional examples of anti-Caucasian prejudices as well as anti-Negro prejudice.[3] Conversely, there is some evidence of excessive desire to avoid the appearance of prejudice. For example, the Negro students report the Caucasian professors are better; the Caucasian students indicate their Negro professors are superior to the non-Negro ones. Although the student body is Caucasian, predominantly, virtually all of the Caucasian students are commuters while most of the Negro students are residential. Nevertheless, the spirit of equality, and of respect and disrespect on an individual basis has been achieved to a high level. (While human-relations literature neglects to mention it, if respect is an individual attribute, a disreputable person should be entitled also to an earned share of disrespect as well.)

In another state university, in a border state, where hundreds of Negro students have begun to enroll, the institution has not yet overcome the impact of their coming. The difficulties of assimilation are much the same as one would find with scores of foreign students who had learned to speak English very well but for whom the language itself was virtually the only recognizable bond. With the best of intentions, a natural resegregation has taken place within the university. With dedicated effort, a cooperative program has been established between that institution and a predominately Negro college in North Carolina.

And so it goes in the desegregation era. The Negro enters the historically Caucasian institution asking himself, "Who am I?"; the Caucasian students and his professors are asking, "We know who we were, but who are we now?" The institution itself continues to struggle with or to ignore its own identity.

Bertram Karon conducted a helpful study, some years ago, concerning the effects of culture, especially regarding the caste system effects of discrimination upon the Negro personality.[4] Prior research had demonstrated the Negro's problems of low esteem, of anger and of anxiety, over being unable to mute or control his feelings of hostility. Karon compared the southern Negro with the northern Negro, based on the assumption that while the northern Negro suffered massive discrimination and implicit threat, he yet enjoyed (in 1958) more freedom from fear than did the southern Negro.

The study was one of careful design, making effective statistical use of sampled populations, and was validated to some extent by a respected projective technique. The study revealed caste sanctions to have a measurable effect upon personality sufficient to account for identifiable differences between Negroes and Caucasians. Karon inferred from his findings that caste sanctions are destructive in direct relation to their severity.[5] They may be, but the explanation is not so simple.

The contrast between northern and southern Negroes was striking. His data, of course, do not tell why. His conjecture was that the northern Negro at least feels free to resent such treatment.[6] He believed that the southern Negro is told by his society that it is wrong to resent mistreatment; that he can never be sure he isn't wrong; but neither can be completely accept such treatment without anger or depression.[7]

If such a contrast were once true, it no longer obtains within the South. The Negro knows that his lot has been one of imposed injustice, and his kindled sense of resentment may cause him to overcompensate for it, especially when he believes that his rights are yielded to him grudgingly.

President Stephen Wright, of Fisk University, dates the birth of the "new Negro" in the South between 1945–50, and reports that he had learned these three bitter lessons:

1. That the white South would never voluntarily dismantle the Jim Crow system . . .
2. That no substantial changes in his status and relationships would ever result from good race relations as they were conceived in the South . . .
3. That the only effective way to change his status was to employ with vigor and imagination the instruments of pressure; the courts, the vote, his economic power, and protests of a variety of types and, further, that any leader who counselled otherwise had outlived his usefulness.[8]

These reports, in combination, alert us to some likely relationships concerning the effects of desegregation in higher education, the cultural conditioning that has preceded this new social context, and the mind sets of Negroes and Caucasians entering into desegregated relationships.

An important part of this initial expectation, and cues to action, stem from the diverse family background of students. The recently released study by the U. S. Department of Labor on the Negro family in America provides some helpful data in understanding some conditions of higher education for Negro Americans.[9] For example, there is little doubt that the matriarchal character of the Negro family explains why so few Negro men ever get to college. Beyond that, the pattern of dissolution of marriages, the fact that a fourth of Negro births are illegitimate, and the dramatic increase in welfare dependency cause us to anticipate two effects of desegregation in higher education.[10] One is a sense of apology for, or shame about, one's family background, just as a poor, culturally disadvantaged Caucasian youth might also feel. The other is the Caucasian students' stereotyped misconceptions about Negro college students' backgrounds which, as middle- or upper-class citizens, are quite different in morals and manners from those of the general Negro population.

These differences in backgrounds, and distorted perceptions of backgrounds, lead us to a further consideration. It has been a frequently observed phenomenon, since the days that William and Mary College recruited Indian Chieftains to become educated to serve their tribes better as leaders, that their education led them, not back to the tribes, but into the white man's world. In current parlance, the dilemma for the Negro is that of achieving a sense of self without "selling out" to the middle-class community.[11] It is a variation of the "passing over" of the light-skinned Negro into the Caucasian world.

The social desirability of light skin among the Negro middle-class illustrates the complex nature of the effects of desegregation. Reflecting this social consciousness, some presidents of predominantly "white-skinned" institutions, in seeking one or two Negro professors, have privately indicated a preference for light skin before indicating the academic teaching fields which they sought to fill.

The matter of changing self-concepts resultant from desegregation is a highly personal affair within an institution. It defies a general answer, and Karon's conclusions have no demonstrably valid relevance for our purpose. Identity hinges upon academic and social success within a given institution by each individual.

One of the most significant studies of the Negro student at predominantly Caucasian institutions of higher learning was that of five "alumni classes" of the National Scholarship Service and Fund for Negro Students (NSSFNS).[12] In recent years, this organization has assisted more than 9,000 Negro students to attend interracial colleges. The study to be described here included a basic population of 509 students among that number, along with incomplete information on 769 others. The investigation was concerned chiefly with matters of academic performance, nonacademic college experiences, and postcollege adjustment.

The initial basic population consisted of 1,519 students. Two hundred forty-one students could not be included because of missing or incomplete transcripts. The findings are further limited since 769 others did not reply to questionnaires forming a part of the study. Even so, the basic facts derived from the study are significant.

Only 18.7% of the respondents and 43.2% of the nonrespondents were college dropouts while approximately 60% of Caucasian students in American colleges and universities drop out. Combining the two Negro groups (which had a measured I.Q. median of 113), the gross dropout rate was 33.4%, roughly equivalent to only half the national average for Caucasians and for Negroes at segregated colleges.[13] These Negro students aspiring to integration, who were less well-prepared academically and financially, managed to complete their baccalaureate program far more consistently than did their Caucasian peers.[14]

Their college grades were average, not distinctive:

> Thirty-one per cent achieved an average of B− or better, and more than 50 per cent achieved C+ or worse for the four years. Slightly less than 10 per cent graduated with honors and about 1 per cent reported election to Phi Beta Kappa.[15]

The dropout rate was lowest and grades were highest at prestige colleges, mainly in the East. The few participating southern colleges reported the highest dropout rate while those from the eastern states reported the lowest. These data are subject to various interpretations. Did the Negroes in the East benefit from preferential consideration; in the South from discriminatory grading? In both cases probably not. The fact is, in any case, that the differences in grades were not statistically significant.

The cause-effect relationships within perceived discrimination are difficult to establish. The facts uncovered in this study were that "the least successful academic group differed from the other groups by reflecting greater racial sensitivity and more hostility towards whites."[16] Such cases could illustrate the frustration-aggression hypothesis. However that may be, the tendency to ascribe causes of limited success to forces beyond ourselves is not a racial, but simply a distinctly human characteristic. As we shall soon see from other studies, however, where Negro students are attempting to study in a climate of social threat, low grades may be directly caused by such socio-psychological discrimination.

An analysis of the Clark-Plotkin study described here would show several limitations from the standpoint of generalizations. The students, in the main, attended institutions outside the South where Negroes were few in number and where the academic and emotional climate was generally supportive. They were a carefully selected group, with reference to motivation, intelligence (authentic I.Q. scores would likely be 120 plus, stripped of ethnic bias) and frustration tolerance. Throughout this experience, they were assured of an abiding interest and of some financial assistance along the way. As the study makes clear, the motivation of the group was exceedingly high, in part influenced possibly by that threadbare cliché, the "Hawthorne effect." From this author's point of bias, the assurance of individuals who personally cared and who could reduce the economic threat of dropout made a crucial difference. The students were "good risks" in every major respect, and they were in minimally threatening collegiate environments, academically and socially.

We cannot safely generalize about the 15,000 Negroes now in predominantly Caucasian institutions from this study, where situations vary from that of hostility to overprotection.[17] The lesson here seems rather that if we are attempting to achieve these general effects, we need to stimulate more of the conditions which appear to be responsible for them. Geographical location per se is clearly not necessarily a significant factor as a variety of studies combine to show. Neither would ethnic ratios seem to be, except insofar as an institution may be unable to provide the academic and social conditions in which Negro students can earn success. The *rate of change* of ethnic ratios could presumably create or compound problems of assimilation, however, in the same way that rapid general enrollment increases sometimes do.

The effects of desegregation need to be viewed in both academic and psychological terms. Both are significant and the two are adjoined by an inseparable interacting bond. This position has been convincingly documented in a number of studies conducted by Irwin Katz and others, and in his review of such studies.[18]

The studies reported by Katz show that social threats, through expressions of hostility or of indifference on the part of Caucasian peers, generate a stress which tends to impair efficiency on relatively complex and difficult tasks, while on simple tasks stress may, on occasion, improve performance. Related to this observable fact is the supporting hypothesis developed by J. W. Atkinson that "the strength of motivation is at a maximum when the probability of success is (perceived to be) 50, and diminishes as this probability approaches zero or unity."[19] If this position is supportable, the Negro entering a new "white standards" environment calculates his chances of success. If he views them as about even, his drive may be at a maximum—which may or may not be the optimum level. That is, if motivation is too high, energies may be expended at the expense of both achievement and mental health. Beyond this, there are individuals who may be classified as "high anxious" or "low anxious" depending upon their degree of frustration tolerance. Unless James Meredith, at the University of Mississippi, or Hamilton Holmes at the University of Georgia, had been capable of absorbing ostracism and sustained harassment, they would have been unable to endure the social threat of their institutional environments, much less achieve academic success. Finally, the question of response to frustration, as a personality pattern variable, should not be overlooked. If Harvey Gantt, the first Negro student at Clemson University, who responded openly and with empathy to an environment of social threat, had been the principal figure at Georgia or Ole Miss, would not the social threat itself have been reduced? A fair amount of evidence would point to such a conclusion, but observers at the Ole Miss scene say it wouldn't have made a—bit of difference.

Studies conducted by Irwin Katz and I. Greenbaum suggest that the performance of Negroes in a desegregated context "may show a wider range of variation in both upward and downward directions than in segregated institutions, depending upon specific features of the situation."[20] In considering the effects of desegregation therefore, the central task is the identification and governing of those "upward" feature conditions.

There are many pieces to the puzzle. Difficulty in expressing aggression openly has been found to correlate with scholastic underachievement.[21] Thus being a "good" Negro in one traditional sense may weaken chances for achieving success, although one may in some instances receive satisfactory grades as a "reward." In the area of testing, when a test administrator is Caucasian, or when comparison with Caucasian peers is expected, Negro subjects tend to become anxious about failure.[22]

Katz' review of research leads him to conclude that when there is a marked discrepancy between what standards require and what students can deliver, the achievement motivation of Negro minority groups is apt to be low because the probability of failure is perceived to be high. Then the *social threat* magnifies, leading to responses of fear, anger, and humiliation that are "detrimental to intellectual functioning." In that manner, a high *failure threat* would be expected to "elicit emotional responses that are detrimental to performance."[23]

Now viewed in positive terms, where hostility and apathy are replaced by good manners and even casual friendliness, where the failure threat is lessened to a "healthy" anxiety level by a realistic assessment of standards and instructional assistance in meeting them, the effects of desegregation upon the Negro student in a predominantly non-Negro environment bid well for academic achievement and personal adjustment. As he is also helped to find socially approved outlets for his frustrations, he will be increasingly able to handle them rather than to bottle them up to a point of explosion or implosion. The effects of desegregation upon the psyche and the academic success of Negro students are both simple and complex. The dilemma is far from being untangled and solved. Yet, a sense of humanity can cut quickly through a maize of discrete scholarly studies. However sophisticated their results, their chief implications are abundantly clear.

REFERENCES

1. Yet in too many cases it is every college for itself and the juniors take the hindmost. The expression is unkind, but the fact is unkinder. Faculty recruitment practices illustrate the point.

2. Broadus Butler, "The Education of the Disadvantaged," paper presented to the 20th National Conference of the Association for Higher Education, Chicago, March 8, 1965.

3. There is probably a two-to-five per cent of "residual constant" of ethnic hostility in southern colleges which cannot be corrected, but must simply be controlled by cultural taboo, and by college regulations and their certain enforcement. For details on the West Vir-

ginia State College situation, see Ponchitto Pierce "Negro Colleges and Integration," *Ebony*, March, 1966.

4. Bertram P. Karon, *The Negro Personality* (New York: Springer Publishing Company, 1958).

5. *Ibid.*, p. 171.

6. *Ibid.*, p. 173.

7. *Ibid.*, p. 175.

8. Stephen J. Wright, "The New Negro in the South," from Matthew H. Ahmann (Ed.), *The New Negro* (Notre Dame, Indiana: Fides Publishers, 1961).

9. Office of Policy Planning and Research, *The Negro Family: The Case for National Action* (Washington, D.C.: U. S. Department of Labor, March, 1965).

10. *Ibid., passim.* With progress in contraception, and increased sexual liberties, the prospect is for increased promiscuity and reduced illegitimacy.

11. William C. Kvaraceus and others, *Negro Self-Concept, Implications for School and Citizenry* (New York: McGraw Hill Book Company, 1965), p. 176.

12. Kenneth B. Clark and Lawrence Plotkin, *The Negro Student at Integrated Colleges* (New York: National Scholarship Service and Fund, 1963).

13. *Ibid.*, pp. 7, 55. The dropout rates of Caucasian and Negro students in segregated colleges in recent years have been closely comparable.

14. *Ibid.*, p. 8.

15. *Ibid.*

16. *Ibid.*, p. 10.

17. In recruiting students to show good faith, the institution risks losing its recognition if too many of them drop out. Thus selective recruitment where standards are high becomes of strategic importance.

18. Irwin Katz, "Review of Evidence Relating to Effects of Desegregation on the Intellectual Performance of Negroes" (ONR Technical Report #8, February, 1964). Also published in *The American Psychologist*, June , 1964.

19. *Ibid.*, p. 6. Thus, if the NSSF students reported by Clark and Plotkin had been less bright or less well prepared, their high motivation might well have been diminished—or they may have "overtried."

20. *Ibid.*, p. 30.

21. *Ibid.*, p. 35.

22. *Ibid.*, p. 36.

23. *Ibid.*, p. 38.

6. The Benefits and Ironies of an Era

Our recent focus of attention has been upon the Negroes who have enrolled in historically Caucasian institutions. That has been a logical central consideration. That has been the initial and continuing focus of attention since the era was begun through legal action initiated by the National Association for the Advancement of Colored People more than a quarter of a century ago. Yet the "side effects" of the era have spread far beyond this direct interest, and they merit our attention along with our concern for the Negro student. Our interest is in the total net societal effects of desegregation, not simply upon Negroes, who, for a host of reasons, have enrolled in historically Caucasian colleges and universities. The field investigations of our Southern Higher Education Study have yielded a good deal of useful information along these lines. What has been reported to us, and what we have seen, form the basis for the observations of this chapter.[1] In the outset the legal right, and to a large extent the moral right of qualified Negroes to enter such institutions has been emphatically assured. The initial purpose of desegregation has been substantially achieved.

The net benefits of desegregation in southern higher education have been good. Negroes entering historically Caucasian institutions have generally been the intellectually elite. They have, in the main, found a satisfying measure of success, which has raised their self-esteem, and has opened new vistas of opportunity to them.[2] Some have faced hostility and indifference; most have found a casual academic friendliness; some others have experienced a full acceptance in the total academic-personal-social college community. Few, indeed, in more recent years have been embarrassed by an excessive pro-Negro treatment. They have tended to move up and out of their social and ethnic origins of deprivation to enjoy their newly earned freedoms. They view their ways of contribution to society more as building an image of the New Negro through career successes and service than in engaging in missionary or liberal reform activities. The more successful they get, the less zeal for militant reform they display.

Negroes in Segregated Colleges

Negro students in the smaller segregated colleges are, in a sense, left behind, but expansion of program and facilities in large state institutions gives a vibrant feeling of contact with the future. Every Negro in a desegregated institution has his counterpart—his equal—in a segregated college or university, but the leadership among Negro students in segregated colleges and universities has been virtually cut in half. Thus the level of motivation, of achievement, and of leadership, has dwindled in the all-Negro colleges, and Negroes feel left out of a movement, but feel an ambivalent insecurity about getting into it. The gap is too great between where they are and where they need to be to avoid overwhelming competition and threat of failure. Negro institutions try to help them bridge that gap. Many Caucasian institutions do not. In the main, the institutions are interested in the superior Negroes, or at least in the ones who can succeed without remedial instruction, or who are outstanding athletes. (Tutorials for athletes may be provided, but no such provision is commonly made for the long-range investment in other disadvantaged, though talented youth.) Like a village that used to be on the main road and is now bypassed by an interstate highway, the Negro is apt to feel his segregated college is bypassed by the new superhighway of higher education unless he sees new life within that institution, too. In many cases he does not.

Caucasian Students Amidst Desegregation

Caucasian students are rearranging their stereotypes of the Negro through desegregation in the predominantly Caucasian colleges and universities. In the main, their prior contacts with Negroes had been with the servant class, the unschooled and subservient domestics. Now they are in contact with another atypical group, the Negro upper- and middle-class, more highly schooled, more intellectual, and far less subservient. Through these contacts a re-education is taking place within and outside the classroom. For one Caucasian group, attitudes of conforming segregationists are slowly shifting from hostility to indifference, and then to an ambivalent friendliness that is not yet sure of itself.

The Caucasian liberals, whose attitudes have sometimes spilled over into a patronizing condescension with its focus on moral responsibility, are learning that Negroes do not wish to be beholden to anyone. Some have helped Negroes to achieve desegregation much as the plantation owner helped his field hands to get out of jail so they could go back to work for him.   Liberals are adjusting to this new equality, however, to find lessons of cultural enrichment through the experience. Without realizing it, some of them felt that "some are more equal than others," and their minds and hearts were not in phase with each other.   They are learning, to their credit, that equal means "just as good and no better," and this lesson in humility is an important effect upon their own liberalized higher education.   This is a new dimension of a liberal arts education, no matter how medieval the curriculum itself may be.

Caucasian Students in Segregated Colleges

The Caucasian student in the segregated college is affected, too.   So long a part of the vociferous majority, he is now a part of the quiescent minority.   He is increasingly uncertain about being in an institution which is left behind.   There are few institutions left for him to go to, and those few are not among the most highly regarded ones.

Even if he regards this flowing social change as moving in the wrong direction, he is not sure he wants to be left behind.   Unlike his segregated Negro counterpart, however, he enjoys a greater freedom to move to a tokenized institution which is in, but not a genuine part of, this era of collegiate desegregation.

Caucasian Students in Predominantly Negro Colleges

Finally, there are the few Caucasian students who have elected to enroll in predominantly Negro colleges.   In a half dozen or so border-state institutions, such as Kentucky State College, Bluefield College (West Virginia) and West Virginia State College, that number is substantial.   Further South, the number dwindles rapidly.   The Caucasian students, in the main, are "imports" from the non-South enrolled in church-connected or private institutions that have considerable financial support from the North and East.

There are many Caucasian students, an indeterminant number within the South, who would like to attend at least for a time or on a part-time basis, a predominantly Negro college.   They are deterred in the first place, because the taboos are strong.[3]   In the second place, there are strong physical threats against it.[4]   Thirdly, what students do, they want to do in concert, not as isolates.[5]   The pressure of social status still runs strong, and Caucasian students, like Negro students, want to make certain that if they attend a Negro college, it enjoys a good reputation in higher education academically, socially, and in interscholastic athletics—if it participates in competitive sports at all.

Effects on the Caucasian Faculty

Since the early 1950's there has been evidence of Caucasian faculty liberality of views concerning student desegregation. When faculty views have not conformed to local community sentiment, this deviance from the community norm has consistently been in the direction of desegregation. Evidence of Caucasian faculty discrimination against Negro students has been extremely rare. On the contrary, some university professors, including several at Duke University and the University of North Carolina, have gone to jail in protest against the segregated eating establishments and other forms of discrimination in or near the collegiate community. Some expressions of liberalism have simply been forms of exhibitionism, but others clearly have not. At schools such as Birmingham Southern College and Millsaps College, a sustained liberal force within the faculty has been influential in the eventual desegregation of the student body.

Efforts to recruit Negro faculty, however, have been sporadic and ineffectual, insofar as faculty action has been concerned. There is no concerted effort to seek candidates without regard to race; more unhappily there are some searching efforts to employ a Negro or two, as a testament to liberality in the South and far beyond it. An impasse in searching for candidates regardless of race is found in the present difficulty of establishing faculty recruitment channels and evaluating the dossiers of prospective faculty members. Beyond this is a kind of haunting fear that if a mistake is made it cannot be corrected in the same way that a Caucasian faculty member could be relieved of his assignment or "helped to find" another position. The concern is that the NAACP would "make a case" out of it.[6]

Again there is the feeling that, under present circumstances, Negro faculty members are at too expensive a premium in rank and salary terms compared with non-Negro instructors of comparable competency. Part of this feeling comes from the fact of the supply-demand situation. Part of it is explained by the equal salary schedules in state institutions which have created a "protected profession" in Negro higher education, one which has suffered from an accumulated heritage of educational disadvantage.

The desegregation era has had virtually no visible effect on recruitment of non-Negro faculty into predominantly Negro colleges and universities except in a few metropolitan areas. Through Woodrow Wilson Fellowships and other similar arrangements, some young Caucasian instructors and others of the junior professional rank serve on a term basis of a year or so, largely from graduate schools of eastern universities. These arrangements, frequently helpful, have not been altogether satisfactory as some individuals, patronizing and almost obsessively upward mobile, have insisted on teaching only graduate or upper division courses, leaving the freshmen and sophomores to the senior Negro professors without the distinction of earned doctorates.[7]

With Caucasian institutions growing too big too fast, the professors have little time now, or inclination, to turn aside from their own career building to take active roles in faculty desegregation—either as ends or means—either in recruitment, or in being considered for recruitment. There is a commitment to institutional liberality, and this commitment is genuine. Personal commitment, however, focuses on doing a good job where one is. Where professors are enabling desegregation to take on a fuller meaning through the service they are performing, is where they appear likely to remain. For the large majority, it is hard to argue against that. It is higher education's "organization man" to remain in the majority group.

Effects on the Negro Faculty

If the general consensus of Negro faculty members could be found, it might be expressed succinctly in such words as these: "I don't want to get out of Negro institutions: I just don't want to feel locked in." Without direct reference to race, there appears generally to be an inverse relationship between age and mobility among faculty members. Thus, the institution that wishes to hold a new faculty member for a decade or more will do better to recruit one past fifty than one under thirty years of age. The senior Negro professor does not care to be uprooted at all, much less to compete on unfamiliar terms, not knowing by what constellation of standards he is to be judged. The senior Negro professor, if he moves at all, is more interested in moving upward in familiar surroundings than in finding a new place in a predominantly Caucasian world.

The more confident young Negro graduate students or college instructors are a bit more responsive to opportunities to enter the desegregated institution as the minority group. In the best of tradition, however, they know they must not appear eager. Such eagerness alone would make conservative Caucasian presidents wary of them.

There are other fundamental reasons. Because of residential segregation practices, Negro professors may be unable to locate in areas where their colleagues generally reside, and they are unsure of their expected social role within the faculty. In a number of cases they would welcome an exploration of this experience if somehow the risk of failure, of personal dissatisfaction, or of loss of face could be minimized. The lines of communication are missing, and no reasonably stable way has been demonstrated to provide this assurance. This is why one college president in a border state said he wanted to employ at least two Negro professors when he employed the first one. A president of a state university searched in vain for qualified available candidates. In Washington, D.C., Howard University is apparently more desirable to Negro professors than is George Washington University.

One unknown variable, causing well-founded concern among some Negro professors, relates to the ominous pattern of biracial institutional "mergers" in which the continuing survival and prospering of public Negro institutions, in whole or in part, will be threatened. The issues are far from simple, and the solutions cannot be simple either. The concern is felt that only perfunctory attention will be given to the varying facets of the problem, and that premature administrative decisions on the state level will prejudice the careers and opportunities of professors for future professional service. However well founded these anxieties, and they are not without foundation, a segment of the faculty in those Negro universities which are located near Caucasian ones are concerned, and some are indignant, about policy decisions which are not maturely derived in the best interest of all college-capable youth, and which are not calculated to make optimum use of all professionally competent faculty members in affected institutions without reference to race.

Effects on the College Administrator

Caucasian presidents who out of moral convictions or from social suasion wish to add Negro members to the faculty, wish to step out boldly—and safely. It is not easy to do both. Very rarely has a predominantly Caucasian southern college employed one or more Negro professors on a continuing basis; fewer than ten in all, according to our inquiries. Dozens of Caucasian presidents would, for a variety of reasons, like to do so. Despite the fact that, in every known instance of such employment, success has greeted the effort, a continuing hesitancy abides. There has been a continuing "grapevine" conversation on long-range strategy and short-range tactics, but the presidents of public and private colleges and universities have not convened to make a concerted study of this issue and to take a forthright position concerning it.

Regarding students, most presidents, regardless of their personal views on desegregation, have come around to it through choice or necessity, and are actively seeking to establish genuine racial harmony, not simply a racial, legalistic truce. The point of most effective entry, some have found, is in the realm of athletics.[8] In one college, for example, six Negro students are enrolled, of whom only one is *not* on an athletic scholarship. In recent desegregation developments, the admission of a few Negro students—and their successful retention—is a clear net fiscal asset in grants and loans in the hundreds of thousands of dollars. Even the legal and fiscal forces, therefore, cause presidents to recognize shifting realities, and to maneuver their institutions on a course to avoid the Scylla of financial distress on the one side, and the Charybdis of educational disruption on the other. They are attempting to make desegregation work in terms of its commonly conceived equal-educational purposes. Some presidents, however, feel yet constrained to convince their conservative supporters that they are doing everything possible to retard or minimize the effort, while persuading the federal government and philanthropic officials that they are moving forward with a crusading liberality. They feel pressed into a dual posture, and surely do not welcome the compromising, anxiety-inducing situation they find themselves facing.

The presidents of predominantly Negro colleges, all or nearly all themselves Negroes, face a far more subtle internal struggle. At this juncture in history, it would be unthinkable for any of them to avoid giving strong public support to desegregation of students and of faculty. Yet, desegregation in the deep South is virtually all a one-way proposition, with no immediate likelihood of predominantly Negro colleges recruiting non-Negro faculty or students—certainly not in the amount of 15,000 of the better ones—as they have "lost" to the predominantly Caucasian institutions. They are caught in the unconscionable squeeze of being victimized by a massive, growing talent search for athletes, for scholarly students, and for promising professors. They can and do call "foul" on other Negro institutions for their raiding practices, but they must applaud in the interest of unilateral desegregation, Caucasian institutions for their raids.

They are comforted by increasing understanding in new forms of federal assistance and foundation support, but this comfort is wrapped up with nonpermanent strings. They wonder about tomorrow. Their professional nobility is being put to the supreme test as they feel the brunt of the negative effects of the desegregation era in southern higher education, while being asked to cooperate themselves out of the best of the educational business. Desegregation has a dear price tag. As one Negro president confided, "The white colleges want the cream, and want us to be challenged by the skimmed milk of academic and athletic talent."

Effects on State, Regional, and National Bodies

The effects go on and on, in ever widening circles, far beyond the South. The effect of alleged police brutality in the arrest of an African student in Tennessee resounds quickly in his home country of Kenya. A visiting group of journalists from several foreign countries talk with Caucasian and Negro students in southern colleges as a basis for subsequent news and feature articles half way around the world.

Within the South, state leaders of the public systems of higher education, however loosely connected or tightly formed, find themselves forced into biracial conjectures as they see colleges and universities growing with almost malignant rapidity. The press for dormitories, classrooms, and degree-holding professors has forced a suspension of effort to achieve progress in program planning and faculty improvement. Colleges are looking first for degrees; secondly for people. Church-connected and private boards of control are likewise drawn away from long postponed considerations of policy and clarity of commitment in higher education.

Regional agencies, such as the Southern Association of Colleges and Schools, the Southern Regional Education Board, and the Southern Education Foundation, are freed now to exercise many leadership options not open to them until the desegregation era achieved considerable progress. The federal government sees the foundation of desegregation it has helped to establish, and wonders how best to build upon it. It must respond to the changes it has been largely responsible for bringing about. Private foundations, seeing much of their traditional function being somewhat happily and massively pre-empted by government intervention, now weigh the questions of their optimum assistance to education and social progress in this emerging postdesegregation era. In the process they get a plethora of public and private advice.[9] The National Association for the Advancement of Colored People, whose political and legal engineering launched the era, must now see the dead end of the legal road ahead, and wonder how to shift its leadership, careful not to lose legal ground, to a higher plateau of a true ethnic community in higher education all across America. Beyond some vaguely defined point, legal pressure yields marginal, if not negative returns.

The desegregation era in Southern higher education, in its commonly employed meaning of assuring access of qualified Negro students into historically Caucasian institutions of higher learning, has at long last neared its conclusion. Since 1948, we have witnessed and have been a part of an era which began with desegregated institutions being an anomaly, and has ended with the segregated institutions finding themselves in a curiously similar category.

The South has turned around, and is confronted with new questions: Where are we going? What is to follow the desegregation era? Will it be an era in which we will come to the end of the rainbow to discover fool's gold, or will we soon find a path to a new level of dignity, of prosperity, and of brotherhood? We cannot say. We can only be sure that unless higher education can find and lead the way, society at large will stumble and bruise itself needlessly and painfully, long before that path is discovered.

The mantle of leadership responsibility has fallen on the shoulders of the higher education community. That community must enlist the sustained yet cautious support of those who wish it well, and who can improve its prospects for success far deeper than the epidermis of higher education. The new era needs to be one in which desegregation is placed in a totally new perspective, where desegregation as an isolated topic is all but forgotten.

REFERENCES

1. "We" refers to the author of this report and to Dr. Harold Stinson, formerly Assistant Director of the Southern Higher Education Study. One of us is Negro; the other, Caucasian. Separately and together, we have listened, observed, and compared our findings.

2. In one historically Caucasian private institution, however, despite careful selected recruitment of several top-ranking Negro students, not one has yet managed to succeed and persevere, in a congenial environment, to baccalaureate graduation.

3. A group of Millsaps College students (Jackson, Mississippi) privately expressed a strong desire to take some courses at nearby Jackson State College, but knew it would "not be looked on with favor."

4. One Caucasian student in Louisiana applied for admission to a Negro college. A cross was burned on his lawn a few nights later. He withdrew his application forthwith.

5. Students in Tennessee have expressed a feeling of wanting their small primary peer group to enroll together, for an interracial educational experience of a "tryout year" in a reputable Negro college.

6. There is, of course, a lesser concern about the American Association of University Professors, "censuring" an institution for unfair dismissal of a Caucasian or Negro professor, but the NAACP's threat is, to some, more powerful and less rational.

7. For a good account of this interinstitutional cooperation, see Bernard

W. Harleston's article, "Higher Education for the Negro," *The Atlantic*, 216:5 (November, 1965), pp. 139–144. The inside stories, from our interviews, reveal cases ranging from deep satisfaction to a disillusionment of major proportion. In the latter instances, administrators are cautious in revealing the nonsuccess lest they impair their goodwill relationships. They swallow their pride, as in the days of segregation.

8. In 1964, expressions of deep concern were heard that desegregation might split the Southeastern Conference apart, causing universities such as Ole Miss to withdraw. Coaches and presidents have stayed "on top of the problem," and desegregation has been accomplished without a serious rift anywhere.

9. Philip M. Stern, "An Open Letter to the Ford Foundation," *Harpers*, 232:1388 (January, 1966), pp. 83–87.

7. The Postdesegregation Era

We have studied the era of desegregation in higher education in its multidimensional character. The term desegregation has been employed in the historical and conventional sense of a nonsegregated establishment without demonstrable discrimination. That era of voluntary and reluctant compliance, with its legal pushes and its economic pulls, has about run its course.

The imponderable question before us is what will the era be like which succeeds it? We in the South face the awesome choice of whether we shall simply drift into this new social age, or whether by resolute action we will help to shape its character. The years of 1966–70 promise to be the crucial years in the making of that decision. Opportunities for action will not be thereafter lost, but they will be significantly lessened with each passing year.

I. SUBSTANTIVE CONDITIONS FOR PROGRESS

Progress in social affairs comes about through a curious combination of personal and organizational effort. No individual can do a great deal alone and without material resources, but he is not impotent alone. Conversely, no organization, public or private, can either dictate or purchase progress without a depth of individual commitment at the point of crucial action. Yet, limited goals can be achieved by the threat of sanction or by the lure of financial advantage. The three major conditions for progress suggested here, and the numerous detailed recommendations following them, consist of an effort to show the interdependence of persons and their humanly contrived organizations in effecting desirable social action in higher education. Beyond that effort is shown how Everyman in higher education can modestly affect social progress through assuming a "first person" responsibility for it.

81

The Condition of Coordinated Effort

To hope for full coordination of effort among hundreds of Southern institutions in behalf of educationally, ethnically, or economically disadvantaged youth is patently unrealistic. Many institutions have other significant goals which would be needlessly weakened by giving major attention to this cluster of problems. Georgia Tech, Rice University, and Duke University, to cite examples, are perhaps among them. They have other unique roles in society. Some other institutions plainly don't care. Yet there is a need for collective effort among the loose systems of higher education, where there is active or latent concern, to focus responsibility for meeting such challenges.

On the local level, in urban communities, increased interinstitutional cooperation is increasingly desirable. Southern Methodist University, for example, makes scholarships available for nearby Bishop College students to enroll for courses. In St. Louis, Missouri, and in a few other cities, a full-time coordinator of higher education is employed to facilitate cooperative effort in every relevant area of higher education. This, and much more, should be striven for in every urban community. Collegiate pacts of mutual assistance should become commonplace in urban communities. We must proceed to cooperate a few blocks apart as well as across the nation and with institutions abroad.

On the state level, the public higher education system should establish its own provisions for accommodating, in one institution or another, all college-capable youth. In this connection, at least two or more institutions (one predominantly Caucasian, the other predominantly Negro) should be designated to perform as models, with ample state support to grapple with problems associated with disadvantages of race, of academic backgrounds, and of financial circumstances.

Similarly, the church-connected and private institutions should act in concert to designate two or more institutions within each southern state where this educational mission could be a kind of unique reason for special support, from religious organizations as well as from private sources.

Interstate cooperation is already immeasurably enhanced by the existing operational mechanisms of the Southern Regional Education Board and the Southern Association of Colleges and Schools. Beyond these organizations, the U. S. Office of Education should establish a regional center to extend its own services to the South, with reference to the Civil Rights Act of 1964, the Higher Education Act of 1965, and to the educational functions likely to be in transit from the Office of Economic Opportunity to the Office of Education, such as Operation Upward Bound. Finally, a privately supported regional center for higher education is needed to complete the requirements for coordinated effort. This proposal is not new, but it is reiterated and altered from previous studies due to its increasing urgency.[1] It might become first established in modest manner as a Center for Higher Education of the Talented Disadvantaged (CHETD). In subsequent years, it should expand its range of research, consultation and regional service, but should not become diverted from this area of responsibility.

With such coordination on local, state, and regional levels, a spirit of common purpose can be accomplished. Without it, discrete isolated efforts will be of little avail, like the desegregation of Berea and Tougaloo Colleges for generations, with no appreciable spread of effect into the mainstream of higher education.

The Condition of Sustained Commitments

Institutions have been sharply denounced on occasion for lack of integrity in living up to their lofty goals. Administrators have been criticized for their status and power seeking; professors for their opportunistic mobility. These charges have some validity in fact. Philanthropic foundations, on the other hand, are periodically criticized for their initial support of ideas and their unwillingness to see them through to conclusion, or for failing to underwrite basic support on which successful educational ventures must rest. They are criticized, too, for their lack of a forthright support of social action in matters of civil rights and race relations.[2] But mutual cooperation, not retaliatory indictment, is what higher education requires.

Foundations now need to identify a few institutions which represent a continuing commitment to the extension of opportunities in higher education, and say to them:

> For a decade, we invite you to become a "foundation-connected college." We want to work with you, through the thick and thin of the next ten years, in advancing opportunities for talented, disadvantaged youth. State and federal support must be sought and utilized maximally, but you can count on us, within moderate limits, to assist your efforts. Ours is a shared, sustained commitment, come Democrats or Republicans, and we join you in common cause.

What has been said about foundations applies equally to church bodies, sectarian or ecumenical. For such bodies to puzzle about the role of church-related colleges, and to neglect to fulfill this urgent need may be to miss the point of the parable of the Good Samaritan. Additionally, each state system must build this assurance of sustained commitment into the pattern of its biennial budgets, or it will be unable to discharge its legal and moral responsibility to all of its citizenry.

The Condition of Desegregation in Perspective

The pattern of attention throughout the desegregation era has been understandably distorted. There has been a tendency to become preoccupied with desegregation to the exclusion of crucially relevant considerations, such as academic and social readiness, or to ignore it altogether, resisting or being unmindful of the inevitable intrusion of ethnic problems upon all major educational decisions in the South.

If the postdesegregation era is to move beyond the present plateau of achievement, the American South and non-South must henceforth avoid dealing with desegregation as an isolated phenomenon, and consider it within the general context of other germane areas of educational opportunity and concern. Students, Caucasian and Negro alike, have a claim upon special consideration if their background and status militate unduly against their chance to become optimally educated. Classification by race will continue to be helpful, on occasion, in fulfillment of higher education functions, but the spotlight must be taken off the racial aspects of higher education. Higher education's homework for tomorrow is to direct our collective energies toward the broader demands of society. If liberal Caucasians and Negroes have nothing in common but a commitment to civil rights and desegregation, they are strangers indeed. The best thing we can do about desegregation in higher education, in this sense, is largely to forget about it except when it emerges as a part of an educational or personal problem.

The conditions of coordinated effort, of sustained commitments, and of desegregation in perspective are the necessary antecedents for substantial progress in the postdesegregation era. The proposals which follow will be strengthened or weakened in the measure that these conditions are attained.

II. PROPOSED COURSES OF ACTION

The following proposals were derived from a wide variety of sources. They came from the Advisory Board of the Southern Higher Education Study. They came from scores of interviews with students, faculty, and administrative officials in Southern colleges and universities. They came from written reactions of the presidents of twenty-one Southern colleges and universities outside of the above groups who gave our questions their unhurried, thoughtful attention. The recent study of *The Predominantly Negro Colleges and Universities in Transition*[3] was helpful as a base for comparing data and in reconsidering some tentative recommendations. Beyond the South, the "Blueprint for Action,"[4] growing out of a "Conference on the Negro" composed of delegates from twelve colleges and universities in the Midwest, provided additional points of useful reference. Nevertheless, the following recommendations represent the sole responsibility of the author. They are based upon the widely shared certainty that a simple removal of ethnic barriers to college admission is insufficient; and full concurrence with the view, as Logan Wilson recently expressed it, that "Higher Education must act much more aggressively and imaginatively."[5]

The higher education picture of desegregation needs to be recognized as being vastly different from that on the precollegiate level. The press for extended desegregation in public school systems continues to be largely stymied even in 1966, despite the Civil Rights Act of 1964, and the formality of compliance with a pharasaic "freedom of choice."[6] "Massive tokenism" continues to prevail on lower levels, but in higher education genuine access is a demonstrable fact in virtually all public institutions and in a large majority of the nonpublic ones. The South needs to see there a model of success, not a reflection of failure, beyond desegregation.

The Precollege Predicament

It is easy for the college and university to blame its problems on the kindergarten, but it is not helpful to do so. Whatever good is accomplished by "Head Start" programs is more than a decade away from higher education. Meanwhile, colleges must seek to assist at the precollegiate level where there is still hope, and still time.

Instruction: Many college instructors of freshmen courses in English, mathematics, and science should teach, in high school, a single regular course or occasional senior class. Frequently, their instruction should be in high schools in which they are in the minority ethnic group. This contact and experience will help high school students who aspire to college, and should be beneficial to college instructors in their own freshmen classes. Such actions may, in addition, facilitate faculty desegregation in public schools.[7]

Counselling: High school counsellors need to obtain and compile, for Negro and Caucasian students alike, reliable information concerning the *social threat* of insitutions in regard to ethnic groups and social class; the *failure threat* in regard to academic attrition, and the remedial or special instruction available to disadvantaged students; and the *financial threat*, along with scholarships, work-study programs, loans, and other benefits available to mitigate it. The counsellor's role is to help each student to measure these deterrents to success, and thus assure a reasonable chance of completing his college education to the normal termination of his plan, whether it be a junior college program or one leading to a baccalaureate degree. In this connection, particular attention should be given to the Negro male student, because of the context of futility in which he has characteristically lived.

Booster Projects: Such booster programs as "Project Opportunity" (of the Ford Foundation and the College Entrance Examination Board) beginning with bright seventh graders, and the "Project Upward Bound" (initiated by the U. S. Office of Economic Opportunity) which provides a kind of last academic precollege chance, are based on sound concepts and have a great deal of merit. All such programs need to be guided, however, by these principles:

1. Their goals must be reasonable in point of amount of disadvantage to be coped with in the time to do it.
2. A continuity of assistance to individual students must be assured. Temporary concern, followed by anonymity, can be both educationally and personally disastrous. (Many programs and short courses have aimed too high and stopped too soon, leaving students bewildered and adrift.)
3. Caucasian and Negro students should be helped without preferential consideration for either group on the basis of race alone. Except in Appalachia, and in other areas of the rural South, however, Negroes will continue to be preponderant among such chronically disadvantaged groups.

Recruitment: Predominantly Caucasian institutions need to become increasingly active in recruiting Negro students who show good promise of success. The 3,000 "commended candidates" of the National Achievement Scholarship Program (the Negro supplementary counterpart of the National Merit Scholarship Program) yields a good list of such prospects. This Program might also do well to publish a list of the next most promising group of 3,000 Negro students who would also be good risks in typical, predominantly Negro or predominantly Caucasian institutions.

A) To assure continuity of desegregation practices in the more reluctant "Compliance" institutions, small groups of Negro students, academically able and socially mature, should be encouraged and enabled to attend these institutions to prevent a regression to segregation.

B) Conversely, the more prestigious and academically demanding among the predominantly Negro colleges should seek to recruit and offer "cluster scholarships" to several southern Caucasian students (at or near the level of National Merit semifinalists) on a one- to four-year basis.

In both the A and B categories, this might be for one year, or for up to four years (first year, $2,000; each year thereafter, $1,000). The plan could also serve as a "Junior year across," an equivalent to the widely established "Junior year abroad" program. Faculty desegregation would, of course, be beneficial in promoting such plans.

No gimmicks, to be sure, will get at the roots of problems. Once having clarified goals and problems attendant to their achievement, however, *specific proposals are necessary as vehicles to goal fulfillment.* The central thesis concerning the precollege years is that we in higher education must not sit limply by and wait for the "head starters" to get to college. Nor can we neglect our duty to secondary schools in the area of instruction, of academic guidance, and of a recruitment and scholarship program consonant with each institution's avowed goals, its admission policies, and its educational programs.

On the College Campus

On each college or university campus, there is a kind of institutional culture that has much in common with other institutions, and much that is unique about it. That corporate personality resides in the character of the students, their sense of purpose and responsibility, their inquisitive and sometimes acquisitive outlook. You talk with them. To find out what a college is like, and to study the nature of the barriers or the doorways to progress, you go—and you listen. But students leave many bewildering gaps. To fill these in, you need to hear the faculty, the administrators, and the unnamed others. They are all a part of that institutional culture.

Within that campus setting, only through mutually supportive action can the efforts of any individual yield their maximum results. Students can often provide the idealistic drive for change; professors are the pivotal persons over the long pull in impeding or effecting it; administrators can provide a fertile or barren soil for progress to flourish or to wither, but they cannot make it grow.

The College Student: If he is a Caucasian, the student facing tomorrow faces a personal inquisitive challenge to give the concept of desegregation a fair chance regardless of his prior views. His mind must be at least ajar to change; he owes it to himself to give social evolution the pragmatic test. If he is secure, he will help the insecure without regard to color. Then he may stop, or he may move into a fuller friendship on the basis of individual bonds of interests. The mature student's mind in the churning present is not being made up by the weight of tradition nor by an uncritical acceptance of change, but in response to the situations of the moment with intelligence, sensitivity, good manners, and puzzlement.

If his epidermis is dark, or if the culture defines a student as a Negro, even though he may be predominantly Caucasian, he, too, needs to be a realistic student of the facts of prejudice, whether it be pro-Negro or anti-Negro in nature. He will not seek to ascribe failure to prejudice when it is due to his own inadequacy or lack of effect. (He knows that half of the Caucasian students will not finish college; that failure is not a race-related phemonenon. But, like others, it will be more "human" to look for causes of failure outside himself. His race may thus come in handy as an explanation of failure in desegregated colleges.)

He may have serious academic or personal problems. He may not. Whichever way it goes, they will not be unique to those of his own race—but he needs a place to go, someone to turn to. The Dean of Students or the Director of Student Personnel must help him to find that place. If his burdens become oppressive, it is his own responsibility to seek out the source of help, not letting his anxieties grow inside him beyond the point of his capacity to handle them. That is why, in every institution, there should be within the student and administrative or faculty "power structure" some individuals who are known to be fully "approachable" regardless of the student's problems, racial or otherwise.

College Student Groups: Student leaders today have an unparalleled opportunity for helping their institutions to move beyond the mere achievement of physical desegregation. Their work needs to be marked by a broader view than simply a consideration of the occasional plights of Negro students or of Caucasian students confronted with race-linked problems. A college Committee of Student Interests, or some such student mechanism, should see to it that legitimate concerns of all individual students are heard, are properly channeled, and are given constructive attention, and that spurious gripes are checked or at least exposed. There needs to be an extension of what has been called, so frequently of late, a "dialogue" among students as well as between students and faculty. Student groups need to evidence a deep concern for problems of student attrition and for the various causes of student dropout, not only for Negroes but for all deserving students in personal, academic, or financial distress.

The efforts of student leadership must be combined with those of student aid coordinators, with directors of student personnel, with deans of students, and with coordinators of faculty advisers. Such student groups can serve effectively, informally and unofficially, as a referral body, and avoid the despair of individuals having to face alone financial, psychological, and academic crises which might otherwise escape the notice of college officials.

In urban areas where several colleges are located, some mainly Caucasian and others chiefly Negro, considerable undeveloped opportunities present themselves for student groups. An intercollegiate urban council, composed of student leaders from the "league" of institutions could be organized. Such a council could provide for a broadening of the sense of unity within higher education. Students may awaken fuller administrative interest in cooperation by their own collective initiative, and in many cases may find deans of students and academic deans most responsive to the prospect.

Cooperation could include the publication of an intercollegiate newspaper prepared by the respective editors of the separate college papers. Such a council could develop joint collegiate programs of a cultural nature, and could publish a calendar of major college events and thus encourage students from any institution to attend functions of neighboring institutions.

The work of such a council might also extend into a consideration of reciprocal options of courses of credit (a quarter or semester student-exchange plan), a consideration of part-time visiting professors from other institutions, and interlibrary usage, along with access to other facilities.

Student groups might serve as collegiate interview teams in high schools to assist students in making college career decisions. This should be more of a guidance than a recruitment service, encouraging those who would likely succeed to find the educational program they seek, and a congenial "culture," and discouraging others.

In the specific areas of teacher education, opportunities for inter-college seminars of student teachers could be explored through student initiative which would enable future teachers to work in desegregated contexts in more natural and secure circumstances. The Civil Rights Acts of 1964 (Title IV, para. 404) can provide financial assistance in such efforts.

Students, individually and collectively, can make use of the support, encouragement, and many resources available to them, if they will think, plan, and act constructively. The challenge of the future in ushering in the postdesegregation era resides to a large degree in the imagination of students, with the understanding and support of faculty and administrative personnel of higher education.

The Faculty: Professors have been criticized for being insensitive to students and callous about instruction, and for paying tribute in the academic marketplace to the standards of success by which they are publicly and privately measured, materially and prestigiously rewarded. Yet these professors would, in the main, agree with the premise that American higher education should attempt "the fullest possible development of the talents of those individuals able to make use of higher education," and that "whatever blocks that development should be repugnant to the University..."[8] Having thus "resolved," however, the course of action is not yet clear.

The professor does need, admittedly, to overcome the culturally prevalent bias that the greatness of an institution (and hence of its professors) is measured by its student selectivity rate, or by its high student failure rate, or its size, or its wealth, or the number of eminent faculty members it can "boast." These are the measures of *reputation for greatness*, but they are not uniformly the indicators of the *character of greatness*. That character, in its humanistic sense, is a measure of the educational change accomplished within students as a result of their total confrontation with college life.[9] Thus the college that is highly selective is successful only as it responds to its challenge of student talent, a talent which may develop or atrophy, a talent which may be put to social or crassly selfish purpose. The college that is largely unselective can achieve greatness through a service that raises the aspirations and achievements of other youth commensurate with their talents. This is where the disadvantaged Negro student, with college success potential, enters the scene of opportunity for the professor.

The Caucasian professor takes justifiable pride, alongside his Negro associate, in the historically liberal position he has taken with reference to desegregation. But now his responsibility is personal. He needs to work either toward a college admissions policy consistent with academic expectation, or an academic expectation consistent with admissions policy. In public colleges, this need for a consistency of expectation results in a mandate to provide, at some point, remedial or "bridge" courses for all college-capable youth, not for Negro students alone, whose academic backgrounds have been so meager.

The individual professor, Negro or Caucasian, can shape the future as he shows helpful interest in the individual student of the present, as he advises his students with information and understanding. He can work in the interest of academic and personal well-being of students in committee deliberations, as a faculty adviser whose interest goes far beyond course schedules and academic probation, and as a person who makes himself increasingly available for nonpedagogical functions in relationship with students. (Some choose the word "encounters.")

The professor can seek a permanent part-time berth on the "freshman faculty" unless his field is too specialized for such service, and can offer to give some senior high school instruction if his college load can be adjusted to permit it. He can encourage, within his department, the review of credentials of new or replacement faculty without reference to race. Like the southern jury system, unless the names are in the box, they are not apt to be considered. He can make known to administrative officials his interest or willingness to enter into a faculty exchange program with other southern institutions, and can work with the faculty, his chapter of the American Association of University Professors, or other appropriate groups, in that general direction. A few professors in any institution can do a great deal at whatever common task they choose to give high priority. Isolated effort, lacking reinforcement, soon falters.

The challenge of the present is for professors to demonstrate in overt, not necessarily dramatic, ways their willingness to be liberal in service as well as exhortation. Such action calls for imagination, sensitivity and perseverance. It calls, perhaps hardest, for living up to the credo of the professor—who "thinks otherwise," who is not bound by the conventional kudos, but is bound to take his examined assumptions along the paths of logic to uncomfortable, but satisfying conclusions.

With this readiness for service, professors can do much, but their potential is limited without administrative coordination and supportive sanction. Thus, the president and his administrative staff, while unable to assure progress, can do a great deal to facilitate and expedite it. Professors collectively, through their institution, their relationships with advisees and all students, can show the way to the "desegregated heart" on the college campus. In many cases they are already doing it.

The President in Company: The president, in matters of policy and its administration, may feel lonely, but he is never really alone. He is in company with his Board of Trustees in matters of policy formulation. He is in company with his administrative staff as he works with the intricacies of management and educational leadership. He tries, with varying degrees of success, to employ able subordinates and to delegate appropriate responsibility and authority to them to fulfill their missions. The president, therefore, is always in company with the inseparable extensions of his office.

The president needs, first of all—and however difficult—to make clear the institution's stance, its *one voice*, on the matter of desegregation, with due sensitivity to students, faculty, patrons, and others who may or may not support that position. No other recommendations can avail much, so long as a deliberate ambiguity or temporizing of position pervades administrative practice. The private segregated college, is, in 1966, not subject to censure for the integrity of its principle if it lives by it without intrusion.

The hypocritical institution is increasingly vulnerable. There is no possibility for a pseudo-desegregated institution to educate for truth. It thus belies its own *raison d'être*. This position refers to the attitude concerning student admission and recruitment, and concerning whatever unwritten regulatory restrictions may be imposed. It refers to the designation of members of college governing boards, considerations as important among predominantly Negro institutions as among the historically Caucasian ones. The Assurance of Compliance should stimulate institutional self-study toward a clarification of the ethical implication of compliance in higher education as public school systems look to colleges for models of leadership.[10] However trite the truism in this dimension of higher education at this point in history, honesty *is* the best policy.

Once the president, his board, and central administrative team have cleared the position of the institution, the desegregated college is ready to forget about desegregation from the standpoint of the inch-by-inch anguish of gradualism, tokenism, and making certain that the "right" things are said to the "right" private audiences. The president, thus unshackled, is free to be his institution's president.

Then this is one of several things a president might consider doing: Actively recruit Negro and Caucasian students who have a reasonable chance of success, and discourage applicants who do not. In public institutions with low admission standards, and high attrition rates, students should be advised of the college's programs with reference to its experience with desegregation, and its special efforts to help students achieve academic success and to avoid dropouts due to financial hardships.

Other cues for administrative leadership refer simply to those conditions which are sound anywhere, but which have special relevance for achieving an ethnic maturity on a college campus—(1) a student personnel and faculty adviser program that combines personal concern and professional expertness; (2) a coordinated student-aid program that helps a student who is willing to work, to shed his anxiety about being a financial dropout; (3) individualized or small group instruction for the academically able whose schooling backgrounds were conspicuously inadequate; (4) a placement program which gives Caucasian and Negro students an "even break" in job opportunities, and assumes in its operations that graduates will be employed without reference to race, not concealing racial identity any more than age, or sex, or place of birth.

The president should establish a "freshman faculty" and charge it with providing first-rate instruction at that level, and with assisting students to achieve college level standards. These professors should not be limited to freshman-level instruction, but should be assigned at least one-third to one-half time on that level. They should hold regular faculty meetings for curriculum study and for the improvement of academic guidance of students. Senior ranking professors should serve on such faculties along with their junior associates.

General faculty recruitment and exchange should be administratively arranged in such a way that every student has an opportunity to elect courses taught by a professor of a different race in his or some other institution. Each faculty should normally include at least three to five professors in a minority group category. In urban communities, arrangements should be made for part-time visiting professors. Such a purpose of desegregation could be accomplished by reciprocal institutional arrangements to register for some courses in neighboring institutions as a part of a regular program. The previously proposed "Junior Year Across" program could accomplish some of these objectives of combining academic and intercultural education.

In urban situations, a full-time coordinator of higher education should be employed by institutions jointly, to facilitate and broaden cooperation in higher education, and to insure attention to desegregation in its broader general context. The president can strengthen his own institution as he is helped through such coordination to work for, not against, his institution's enlightened self-interest.

The president who can muster sufficient initial support from his constituency can serve the cause of Southern higher education exceedingly well by repudiating the conventional claims to greatness. He can lead his college resolutely toward evolving a miniature democracy in which higher education can flourish with a minimum of "social threat" by encouraging healthy race and social relations; of "failure threat," by helping students achieve attainable standards; and of "financial threat," by arranging for students to be assured of adequate resources through scholarships, labor, and loans. The South is in sore need of a few public and nonpublic institutions like this to "look at" from all around the nation, the "Lambarenes" of higher education.

Beyond the Campus

Leadership on state, regional, and national levels has a strategic role in effecting improvement, and in precluding fragmentation of effort at the institutional level. This point has been stressed earlier, and requires only brief additional comment here in explicit terms.

State Leadership: In the public sphere, the selection of new college presidents must be a point of major concern. The "program" oriented president, rather than the "edifice" or "hotel" oriented president, will bring about the improvements on matters of our concern. Without deliberately seeking to desegregate on the leadership level, presidents of predominantly Negro institutions should, in some instances, be appointed without regard to race, as was the legal counsel of the NAACP. New presidents of all institutions should be favorably disposed toward selecting central administrative staff without regard to race.[11]

Standards for college admission should require a minimum of either tenth or eleventh grade achievement level, until high school diplomas can assure that achievement level. For students to be in "college," while four to six years below college level, needlessly adulterates the meaning of higher education. Delayed college placement and remedial instruction should enable students to come within "hailing distance" of a college education before being admitted to it. Interim programs should be provided in colleges or on selected secondary school campuses.

In the merger of institutions, predominantly Negro institutions must not be expediently merged with or swallowed by those which are historically Caucasian. Though only blocks apart, they may be years apart in admissions standards, and in program offerings. In some cases, a predominantly Negro institution might properly become a desegregated, distinctive community college for the educationally talented but disadvantaged. A terminal program of vocational, technical, and general education might be provided, with doors open to the other institution for students whose aptitude and achievement warrant such higher education—a "staging area" in higher education.[12]

Regional Leadership: It would be presumptuous to suggest what specific regional agencies might do to advance educational opportunities in the postdesegregation era. The Southern Regional Council, the Southern Education Foundation, the Southern Association of Colleges and Schools, the Southern Regional Education Board, and the Southern Education Reporting Service are each viewing the changing scene vigilantly to discern cues for their exercise of unique appropriate educational and social leadership. It is hoped, however, that the Southern Association might see fit to focus upon these endemic problems related to race and poverty at an early date, either in terms of convention emphasis or through study groups of its College and Secondary School Commissions. In addition, some coordinated study and action by the above agencies, all but one headquartered in Atlanta, might now prove useful. In addition, these agencies, separately and collectively, can be beneficial both to governmental and private agencies which seek to improve the character of southern higher education with some special concerns about the plight of promising Negro students related to or independent of the issues of desegregation.

National Leadership: The Association for Higher Education (of the National Education Association), the American Association of University Professors, and the American Association of School Administrators all have a potentially important leadership role to play, because the postdesegregation era is one the nation is entering together. Our present attention is limited, however, to the roles of the federal government and to private philanthropic foundations.

The Federal Government: Despite saturation spending mistakes, the Department of Health, Education, and Welfare is worthy of commendation for its efforts toward equal education opportunity, its work-study program, its Upward Bound Project, and others. It has moved massively, constructively, and rapidly, and this is only the beginning, judging from the Higher Education Act of 1965. In this ambitious program, to maximize the spread of its success and to minimize the effects of failure, these suggestions seem relevant in 1966.

1. Do not press hard for maximum desegregation, but work toward ethnic integration where desegregation in reasonable measure has been accomplished. Concentration on desegregation is in order, of course, where the Assurance of Compliance appears to be in bad faith.

2. Study and evaluate the numerous efforts initiated by private foundations to ascertain which have the greatest prospect for success when duplicated on a grand scale.

3. Initiate research, demonstration, and evaluation centers for each major project now undertaken on a long-range basis. Thus, a "working model" should be under close scrutiny while extensive evaluations are being made of its numerous variations from one institution to another. Where evaluations are now "farmed out" might be a good beginning point, as in Civil Rights Educational Institutes.

4. One-year staff recruitments from American colleges and universities should be expanded to provide constant, competent advisory services and to increase field observations and the consultant services regarding such matters as student aid, desegregation, remedial instruction, and student personnel services. Professors and administrators unwilling to accept a long-

term appointment would accept such an assignment, and some could render distinguished service in it.

Foundations: Private philanthropy is both relieved and concerned at the way its traditional role has been pre-empted by the federal government. It has been relieved by the massive furtherance of some of its own objectives. It has been concerned about the uprooting effects of some hastily contrived efforts to solve with panacea-like patterns some problems whose roots go very deep indeed. What a foundation can now do to be of most help to higher education beyond desegregation depends, of course, upon its resources and the special nature of its objectives. Among many possibilities, these salients of opportunity are illustrative:

1. Short-range action programs, in colleges and senior high schools attempting to move "beyond desegregation," should be encouraged and supported, especially where such efforts could be reasonably well evaluated, and where they showed promise of a spread of effect if taken over subsequently by governmental agencies.

2. Scholarships to Caucasian and Negro students enrolled in institutions of a predominantly different race should be provided with an established assurance to students of continued interest and support, similar to that now under the aegis of the National Scholarship Service Fund, but expanded and available without racial preference. The "Junior Year Across" idea would be one example. The "cluster scholarship plan," for Caucasian or Negro high school seniors, would be another.

3. "Faculty differential scholarships," to encourage temporary faculty assignments of one year or less, in an ethnically opposite institution should be provided. (For example, if a professor earning $12,000 accepted a $9,500 assignment, the foundation scholarship would provide the difference, and a small salary increase and added actual expenses for travel and housing accommodations.)

4. The larger foundations should "spot survey" a number of the promising nonprestige institutions (historically Caucasian and historically Negro) and enter into a long-term commitment of general assistance to a few of them to focus on the "threats" in higher education, the social, financial, and academic deterrents to success. An initial basic grant should be given, unrestricted, with subsequent grants to be based on the use of the original grant and the college's plans for continuing educational development and service. This refers to the "foundation-con-

nected college" idea suggested earlier, whatever other "connec-
tions" a college may have.

The opposing argument, of course, is that a foundation should
not "control" a college. This is true, which makes it doubly
important from the beginning that the college make a genuine,
not an opportunistic, commitment to stay with the problem
areas identified, and that the foundation, within generally fixed
commitments, have faith in the institution, but exercise continuing care that this be a genuinely cooperative enterprise in
an authentically common cause, not one which will easily be
diverted.[13]

5. *For continuity and coordination of effort, an independent national center
of research and service should be established within the deep South to focus
its attention on higher education problems and opportunities related to
race, to poverty, and to precollegiate educational disadvantage.* Located
in Atlanta, Nashville, New Orleans, or the "Triangle" N.C., it
could be attached to two institutions, one predominantly Negro,
the other chiefly Caucasian. With a small biracial staff, it
should conduct needed inquiries of importance to colleges and
schools, serve as a clearing house in matters of student recruitment and special faculty placement, along with other relevant
concerns of higher education, and provide or arrange for con-
sultative services to senior high schools and colleges on a no-
cost or low-cost basis. In addition, it could serve a continuing
advisory function to governmental, philanthropic, and church-
related agencies.[14]

III. THE END AND THE BEGINNING

The desegregation era in higher education was characterized by
turbulence, and the previous chapters have contained the epilogue of
that uneasy era. The postdesegregation era is marked by an ominous
quiescence, and that era has just begun. Now there is a new turbulence
across the land in American higher education. Its diagnosis is "Proposal
Sickness," and it is a contagious disease. Good men and good women,
Caucasians, Negroes, and others are writing proposals for federal and
private grants guided by opportunism. Hasty decisions are being forced
on matters of judgment requiring careful deliberation, and money
changers are aborting many long-range goals of higher education.

With this new turbulence and this new quiescence, one cannot look
to the future without misgivings about it. The future we will find is the
one that we ourselves are making. With our actions, we are writing
the prologue to the postdesegregation era for all of American higher

education. Posterity will study this early shaping of an era with unusual interest, especially the role of the educated, the affluent, and their collegiate institutions.

The student, meanwhile, depends upon the professor, and he upon his president. The president leans, in turn, upon his governing board, his government, and other supporters and controllers—foundations, church-related organizations, the important business world and the opinion-forming press. But dependence works both ways. The government depends upon college officials for implementing its many worthy objectives. Sometimes it has to show a faith in presidents it doesn't really "believe in." Foundations, as well, would be well advised to terminate their giving unless institutional donees could be found which showed promise of goal achievement. College presidents and deans are administrators who facilitate the academic and social action of their subordinates, and are crippled in their efforts without able and loyal ones. Enlightened self-interest mandates an upward and a downward loyalty, and demands the assumption of a personal, individual responsibility for change.

To conclude, then, or to begin, we—you and I—must not be "virtuously blind," nor "shrewd to bad purposes," but, as Benjamin Vaughan expressed it two centuries ago, we must strive to put under our hand only those matters that we deem to be at the same moment wise, practical, and good. There is nothing new about the idea, except the current ways which we can discern to give it creative, constructive expression; and the will to do it.

REFERENCES

1. In 1961, the Commission on Goals, of the Southern Regional Education Board, recommended one or more centers for the study of higher education. In 1965, Earl McGrath's study of predominantly Negro colleges and universities recommended a center to provide counselling and field services to those institutions. In 1966, a current adaptation of these proposals is more important than ever. A recommendation need not be new to be valid.

2. Philip Stern recently took the Ford Foundation to task for not supporting the Urban League and the Southern Regional Council (see "An Open Letter to the Ford Foundation," *Harper's*, 232:1388, [January, 1966], pp. 83–87). He did not mention multimillion-dollar grants to the Southern Education Reporting Service, and the Southern Association of Colleges and Schools, nor how that Foundation had been excoriated for withholding consideration of grants to segregated institutions. Those are the "other realities."

3. Earl J. McGrath, *The Predominantly Negro Colleges and Universities in Transition* (New York: Institute of Higher Education, Teachers College Press, Columbia University, 1965).

4. Institute of Human Relations, *Blueprint for Action by Universities for Achieving Integration in Education* (Milwaukee: University of Wisconsin, 1964).

5. *Ibid.*, unnumbered "Comments."

6. "School Desegregation: Old Problems Under a New Law" (Atlanta: Southern Regional Council, September, 1965). Less than 6% of Negro Southerners enrolled in public schools are in desegregated schools in the eleven states of the Old Confederacy. The U.S. Office of Education estimates that 24,500 Negroes are in desegregated classes in North Carolina. The Southern Regional Council estimates one-third that number. In Alabama, the U.S. Office estimate is 1,530. The Council can locate only 717 (pp. 4–5). The U.S. Office necessarily compiles reports received from school systems. Other agencies use less optimistic, but sometimes more reliable, data.)

7. Harold Stinson wisely cautions that the mere recommendation that professors do some high school teaching is not enough. With it they need to develop ways of teaching high school pupils and college freshmen with varied socio-economic backgrounds.

8. *Blueprint*, op. cit.

9. This view does not contradict, but complements the need for emphasis upon the essential research functions of any true university, which may be relatively separate from collegiate student considerations.

10. The official explanation of the Assurance of Compliance is contained in the appendix to this study because of its significance in this regard.

11. In a culture-free logical sense, what applies in a predominantly Negro institution should apply, identically, in a predominantly Caucasian one. In a cultural sense, this is not yet true. Efforts should be directed toward bringing together the cultural and logical lines of reasoning and action. It takes time, but time alone is neutral about the matter.

12. This proposal was offered privately by a leading university dean who said that, while the idea is sound, it would be unable to gain popular acceptance. But progress demands a mature facing of uncomfortable facts about southern higher education.

13. Colleges need some assurance of sustained support beyond the possible vagaries of current political fortunes, a wind which may shift

to some other preoccupation in coming years. There need to be a few anchors of permanent commitment.

14. The USOE Feasibility Study for Regional Educational Laboratories, by Ray Carpenter and others, is a hopeful sign. A recent grant of $300,000 from the Carnegie Corporation to the Southern Regional Education Board, to assist predominantly Negro colleges, is another. The major step remains to be taken while *tempus fugit*.

Appendix

Explanation Of

**HEW FORM NO. 441, ASSURANCE OF COMPLIANCE WITH
THE DEPARTMENT OF HEALTH, EDUCATION, AND
WELFARE REGULATION UNDER TITLE VI OF THE
CIVIL RIGHTS ACT OF 1964**

Section 80.4 of the Department of Health, Education, and Welfare's
Regulation effectuating Title VI of the Civil Rights Act of 1964 requires
that every application to the Department for Federal financial assistance
shall contain or be accompanied by an Assurance that the program or
facility to be assisted will be conducted or operated in compliance with
Title VI of the Civil Rights Act and with all requirements imposed by
or pursuant to the Department's Regulation.

Section 80.4 further provides that "the form of the foregoing Assurance and the extent to which like Assurances will be required of subgrantees, contractors, transferees, successors in interest and other
participants," shall be specified by the responsible Department official.
Under this authority, HEW Form No. 441 has been specified as the
form of Assurance which shall apply to all applications for Federal
financial assistance (except for continuing state programs which must
meet the requirements of Section 80.4(b) and school districts availing
themselves of Section 80.4(c) of the Regulation) submitted to the Department after January 3, 1965; also the circumstances have been specified under which an Applicant shall obtain comparable written Assurances of compliance from its subgrantees, contractors, and transferees. (See answers to Questions 11 and 12 below in this regard.)

HEW Form No. 441 constitutes a legally enforceable agreement
to comply with Title VI of the Civil Rights Act of 1964, and with all
requirements imposed by or pursuant to the Regulation of the Department of Health, Education, and Welfare issued thereunder. Applicants
are urged to read the Department's Regulation before executing the
Assurance.

The following explanation of the requirements of the Department's
Regulation and the examples of the kinds of discriminatory practices
prohibited by them are for the guidance of the Applicants.

101

1. *By executing the Assurance (HEW Form No. 441), what does an Applicant agree to do?*

A. The Applicant agrees to make no distinction on the ground of race, color, or national origin in providing to individuals any service, financial aid, or other benefit under any program receiving Federal financial assistance extended to the Applicant by the Department.

2. *What is meant by "distinction on the ground of race, color, or national origin"?*

A. "Distinction on the ground of race, color, or national origin" includes (1) any type of segregation, separate or different treatment, or other discrimination on that ground; (2) the imposition of any admission, enrollment quota, eligibility, or other requirement or condition which individuals must meet in order to be provided any service, financial aid, or other benefit under a program or to be afforded an opportunity to participate in a program, if the race, color, or national origin of individuals is considered in determining whether they meet any such requirement or condition; (3) the use of membership in a group as a basis for the selection of individuals for any purpose, if in selecting members of the group there is discrimination on the ground of race, color, or national origin; and (4) the assignment of personnel to provide services, or the assignment of times or places for the provision of services, on the basis of the race, color, or national origin of the individuals to be served. It does not, however, include distinctions on the ground of race, color, or national origin determined by the responsible Department official to be necessary to the conduct of research or experimental programs having as their primary objective the discovery of new knowledge concerning special characteristics of particular racial or other ethnic groups.

3. *What is meant by "service, financial aid, or other benefit?*

A. "Service, financial aid, or other benefit" under a program receiving Federal financial assistance includes any education or training, any evaluation, guidance, counseling, or placement service, any health, welfare, rehabilitation, housing, or recreational service, any referral of individuals for any of the foregoing services, any scholarship, fellowship or traineeship stipend or allowance, and any loan or other financial assistance or benefit (whether in cash or in kind), which is made available to individuals (1) with the aid of Federal financial assistance, or (2) with the aid of the Applicant's or of other non-Federal funds required to be made available for the program as a condition to the receipt of Federal financial assistance, or (3) in or through a facility provided with the aid of Federal financial assistance or the non-Federal matching funds referred to in (2).

4. *What requirements are placed on the use of facilities?*

A. The Applicant agrees to make no distinction on the ground of race, color, or national origin in making available to individuals the use of any land, building, equipment, or other facility leased, acquired, constructed, improved, or equipped with the aid of Federal financial assistance extended to the Applicant by the Department, including—

    (*a*) the use of any room, dormitory, ward, or other space in the facility;

    (*b*) the use of any equipment in the facility;

    (*c*) the use of any office, waiting room, restroom, eating, recreational, concession, or other accommodation or convenience provided in the facility;

    (*d*) the use of any facility not provided with the aid of Federal financial assistance if the availability of such facility is required as a condition to the receipt of Federal financial assistance for the Federally-assisted facility.

5. *What requirements are placed on the opportunities to participate in a program receiving Federal assistance?*

A. The Applicant agrees to make no distinction on the ground of race, color, or national origin in affording opportunities to individuals to participate (other than as employees) in any program receiving Federal financial assistance extended by the Department to the Applicant, including opportunities to participate—

    (*a*) as providers of any service, financial aid, or other benefit to individuals under the program (e.g., as physicians, surgeons, dentists, or other professional practitioners seeking the privilege of practicing in a Federally-aided hospital or other facility),

    (*b*) as conferees, observers, consultants, or advisers, or as members of advisory or planning groups, or

    (*c*) as volunteers (e.g., as voluntary workers, or as patients or other subjects of study or experimentation in research, survey, demonstration, or like programs).

6. *Does that mean that an Applicant who signs the Department's Assurance may nevertheless make distinctions among his employees on the basis of race, color, or national origin?*

A. Title VI of the Civil Rights Act does not concern itself with employment practices except where a primary objective of the Federal financial assistance is to provide employment. Thus, where a basic objective of the program is to provide employment, the Applicant's employment practices are subject to the Department's Regulation. However, even where this is not the case an Applicant may be precluded from engaging in any discriminatory employment practices under the provisions of Title VII of the Civil Rights Act, Executive Orders 10925 and 11114, and the Merit System Regulations.

7. *When an Applicant's employment practices are covered by the Department's Regulation, what requirements must be met?*

A. The Applicant agrees to make no distinction on the ground of race, color, or national origin in its employment practices (including recruitment or recruitment advertising, hiring, layoff or termination, upgrading, demotion, or transfer, rates of pay or other forms of compensation, and use of facilities) with respect to individuals seeking employment or employed under any program receiving Federal financial assistance extended to the Applicant by the Department, in those programs where a primary objective of the Federal financial assistance is to provide employment to such individuals. This includes programs under which the employment is provided—

(*a*) as a means of extending financial assistance to students or to needy persons,

(*b*) to students, fellows, interns, residents, or others in training for related employment (including research associates or assistants in training for research work), or

(*c*) to reduce unemployment or to provide remunerative activity to individuals who because of severe handicaps cannot be readily absorbed in the competitive labor market.

8. *What effect will the Regulation have on a college or university's admission practices or other practices related to the treatment of students?*

A. An institution of higher education which applied for any Federal financial assistance of any kind must agree that it will make no distinction on the ground of race, color, or national origin in the admission practices or any other practices of the institution relating to the treatment of students.

(*a*) "Student" includes any undergraduate, graduate, professional, or postgraduate student, fellow, intern, student, or other trainee receiving education or training from the institution.

(*b*) "Admission practices" include recruiting and promotional activities, application requirements, eligibility conditions, qualifications, preferences, or quotas used in selecting individuals for admission to the institution, or any program of the institution, as students.

(*c*) "Other practices relating to the treatment of students" include the affording to students of opportunities to participate in any educational, research, cultural, athletic, recreational, social, or other program or activity; the performance evaluation, discipline, counseling of students; making available to students any housing, eating, health, or recreational service; affording work opportunities, or scholarship, loan or other financial assistance to students; and making available for the use of students any building, room, space, materials, equipment, or other facility or property.

9. *Does the Assurance of nondiscrimination apply to the entire operation of an institution?*

A. Insofar as the Assurance given by the Applicant relates to the admission or other treatment of individuals as students, patients, or clients of an institution of higher education, a school, hospital, nursing home, center, or other institution owned or operated by the Applicant, or to the opportunity to participate in the provision of services, financial aid, or other benefits to such individuals, the Assurance applies to the entire institution. In the case of a public school system the Assurance would be applicable to all of the elementary or secondary schools operated by the Applicant.

10. *What about a university which operates several campuses?*

A. Section 80.4(d)(2) of the Regulation provides for a more limited Assurance only where an institution can demonstrate that the practices in part of its operation in no way affect its practice in the program for which it seeks Federal funds. This would be a rare case.

11. *If an Applicant intends to make use of other individuals to help carry out the Federally-assisted program, does the requirement not to discriminate apply to such a subgrantee or contractor?*

A. It does. The Applicant must require any individual, organization, or other entity which it utilizes, to which it subgrants, or with which it contracts or otherwise arranges to provide services, financial air, or other benefits under, or to assist it in the conduct of, any program receiving Federal financial assistance extended to the Applicant by the Department, or with which it contracts or otherwise arranges for the use of any facility provided with the aid of Federal financial assistance for a purpose for which the Federal financial assistance was extended, to comply fully with Title VI of the Civil Rights Act of 1964 and the Regulation of the Department of Health, Education, and Welfare issued thereunder.

12. *Must this Assurance of nondiscrimination by the subgrantee, etc., be in writing?*

A. In the case (1) of any contractual or other arrangement with another such individual or entity which will continue for an indefinite period or for a period of more than three months, (2) of any subgrant, or

(3) of any conveyance, lease, or other transfer of any real property or structures thereon provided with the aid of Federal financial assistance extended to the Applicant by the Department, the Applicant shall obtain from such other person, subgrantee, or transferee, an agreement, in writing, enforceable by the Applicant and by the United States, that such other individual or entity, subgrantee, or transferee will carry out its functions under such subgrant, or contractual or other arrangement, or will use the transferred property, as the case may be, in accordance with Title VI of the Act and the Regulation will otherwise comply herewith.

13. *What obligations does the Applicant have to inform beneficiaries, participants, and others of the provisions of the Regulation?*

A. The Applicant must make available to beneficiaries, participants, and other interested persons information regarding the provisions of the Regulation and protections against discrimination provided under Title VI of the Civil Rights Act. The Department will issue shortly more detailed instructions on carrying out this phase of the Regulation.

14. *What obligations does the Applicant have to keep records and to make them available to the Department?*

A. From time to time, Applicants may be required to submit reports to the Department, and the Regulation provides that the facilities of the Applicant and all records, books, accounts, and other sources of information pertinent to the Applicant's compliance with the Regulation be made available for inspection during normal business hours on request of an officer or employee of the Department specifically authorized to make such inspections. More detailed instructions in this regard will also be forthcoming from the Department in the near future.

15. *Must separate Assurance forms be filed with each application?*

A. As a general rule once a valid Assurance is given it will apply to any further application as long as there is no indication of a failure to comply.